Clipper Shi
Voyages of Aberdeer

James Mackl

Cover Image
The Clipper Ship Brilliant
by
Artist Montague Dawson

Table of Contents

Introduction....3
Family Portrait....4
The Pension Application Form....5
Setting the Scene - Victorian Aberdeen....7
James' Early Years....11
Apprenticeship Age 13 to 22....15
Marriage....16
Aberdeen Shipbuilding in the mid 1800s....17
The Brilliant (Ship Number 77437)....21
The Ethiopian (Ship Number 48859)....50
The Ballochmyle (Ship Number 67930)....60
The Sophocles (Ship Number 77455)....75
The Soudan (Ship Number 91182)....85
The Last Commercial Windjammers....100
James Later Life....101
Agreement and Account of Crew....104
Credits....155

Revision Status:

1st Edition 14th May 2023

Introduction

This book is a tribute to my great-grandfather James Mackland, who was born in Aberdeen, Scotland in 1858. He was a sailmaker on some of the fastest and most graceful sailing ships of the late 1800s, several of which were built in the Aberdeen shipyards of Walter Hood and John Duthie.

I remember some of the stories told to me by my grandmother when I was a child where she recounted the bravery and hardship her father encountered on his long voyages, many over a year in duration.

With the help of my cousin Lesley (Sutherland) Birnie, I have managed to piece together some remarkable details of a few of his voyages in which he circumnavigated the world. The initial material was obtained from an application form he completed for a seaman's pension in 1929. Sadly, his log books and most of the detailed material relating to his voyages has been lost over the years. The poorly preserved pension application form is the only record that remains of a remarkable life at sea.

My grandmother Mary Ann (Mackland) Sutherland, told me stories about her sailmaker father and the clipper ships he sailed on. She remembered as a child that her father was away from home for long periods of time. On his return from these long trips, she had clear memories that he was paid in gold sovereigns; his return home must have been a very special time for the family.

I am sure that several ships were spoken about, but the one that stuck in my mind was the Ballochmyle, in which he sailed to Australia, then on to Portland, Oregon in the USA, returning via Cape Horn in South America.

One particular trip she remembered her father speaking about was around the Cape of Good Hope in South Africa where he was asked to climb to the top of the rigging during a fierce storm to make safe the sails, in doing so his brave efforts saved the ship. When he made it back to the safety of the deck, the captain took him to his cabin and told him that he hadn't expected him to survive the climb up the rigging. To show his appreciation the captain gave him special thanks, and a very large glass of whisky. This could have been on his second voyage on the Brilliant where they encountered a fierce storm on route to Australia, details are included in the Passage Report.

There was also mention by my grandmother that James had served on the White Star Line ship, the Thermopylae, however to date I have been unable to locate any documentation to support this.

Family Portrait

James Mackland 1858 - 1937
Agnes (Robertson) 1866 - 1928

Agnes and James Mackland

The Pension Application Form

This overlooked, dogeared, faded pension application form unlocked the inspiration to write this book. It gave me the basic information required to piece together some of the voyages James made around the world, on several of the most majestic clipper ships of the closing decades of the 19th century.

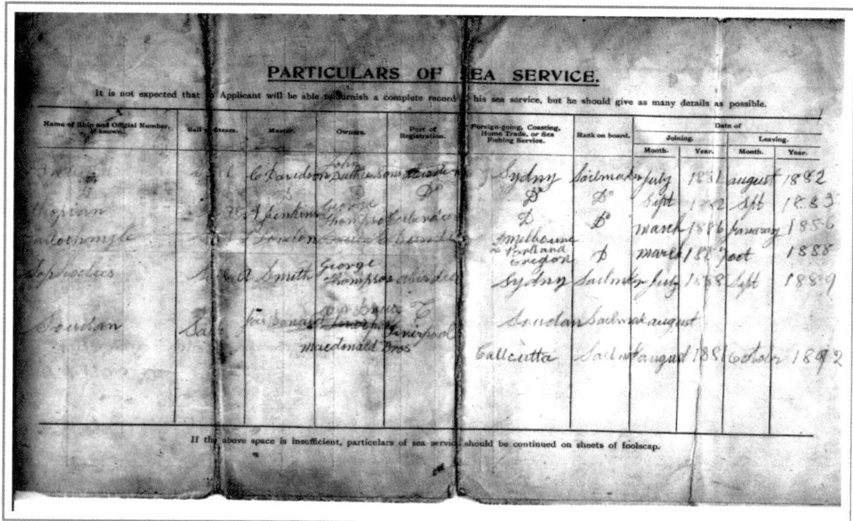

PARTICULARS OF [illegible]EA SERVICE.

It is not expected that [illegible] Applicant will be able [illegible]urnish a complete record [illegible] his sea service, but he should give as many details as possible.

Name of Ship and Official Number, if known.	Sail or Steam.	Master.	Owners.	Port of Registration.	Foreign-going, Coasting, Home Trade, or Sea Fishing Service.	Rank on board.	Date of Joining Month.	Date of Joining Year.	Date of Leaving Month.	Date of Leaving Year.
[illegible]	[illegible]	C. Davidson	John [illegible] Sons	[illegible]	Sydney	Sailmaker	July	1881	August	1882
[illegible]		D°	[illegible]	D°	D°	D°	Sept	1882	Sept	1883
[illegible]	[illegible]	A. Jenkins	George Thompson	Aberdeen	D°	D°	March	1886	January	1886
[illegible]	[illegible]	[illegible]	[illegible]	[illegible]	Melbourne & Portland Oregon	D°	March	188[illegible]	Oct	1888
Sophocles	[illegible]	[illegible] Smith	George Thompson	Aberdeen	Sydney	Sailmaker	July	1888	Sept	1889
Soudan	Sail	[illegible]	[illegible]	Liverpool	Soudan	Sailmaker	August			
			Macdonald Bros		Calcutta	Sailmaker	August	1891	October	1892

If th[illegible] above space is insufficient, particulars of sea servi[illegible] should be continued on sheets of foolscap.

Pension Claim Form

From this document we have managed to produce details of an important part of working life at sea. The application was made under the Lascar Fund, which had been set up as part of the National Health Insurance Scheme of 1911.

The fund required shipowners to contribute towards the pensions for British seamen who had served in the foreign merchant service. This fund later became The Seamen's Pension Fund and subsequently after receiving the grant of Royal Charter in 1931, it became The Royal Seamen's Pension Fund.

James' service record listed in the application gave details of the clipper ships he served on after completing his apprenticeship. From this single document we find that James first went to sea, in foreign service, as a sailmaker in 1881, at the age 23, after serving a long apprenticeship in Aberdeen as a rope and sailmaker. During his apprenticeship he will have gained first hand experience working on local sailing ships.

The vessels listed in the pension form are mostly iron hulled clippers, built for the Australia wool trade. These vessels would have been the state of the art of high speed sailing ship construction.

The poorly preserved document was first digitised, then photographically enhanced to bring out as much detail as possible of the almost illegible hand writing, this allowed me to transcribed the information into a working spreadsheet. As the material was researched more blanks were filled in.

Name of Ship	Sail or Steam	Master	Owners	Port of Registration	Foreign going, Coastal, Home Trade or Sea Fishing Service	Rank on Board
Brilliant	Sail	C Davidson	John Duthie Sons	Aberdeen	Sydney	Sailmaker
Brilliant	Sail	C Davidson	John Duthie Sons	Aberdeen	Sydney	Sailmaker
Ethiopian	Sail	A Jenkyns	George Thompson White Star Line		Sydney	Sailmaker
Ballochmyle	Sail	Louden	David Bruce	Dundee ?	Melbourne then Portland Oregon	Sailmaker
Sophocles	Sail	A Smith	George Thompson White Star Line	Aberdeen	Sydney	Sailmaker
Soudan	Sail	Jas Donald	Macdonald Bros	Liverpool	Calcutta	Sailmaker

The ships listed included:

Ship	Departure Port	Captain
The Brilliant	London	Davidson
The Ethiopian	London	Jenkins
The Ballochmyle	Dundee	Lunden
The Sophocles	Aberdeen	Smith
The Soudan	Liverpool	Donald

The information provided enough material to start the internet search which would ultimately lead me on a multi year investigation uncovering some remarkable details about his voyages, and the ships he sailed on.

It became evident that some of the dates listed on the pension form didn't quite match with the material which was later uncovered from crew lists, and press articles. The definitive material came directly from the copies of the original Crew Agreements.

Many of the organisations contacted were extremely helpful in permitting the use of their material to give meaningful context to the voyages and events that were uncovered.

Setting the Scene - Victorian Aberdeen

Aberdeen in Victorian times had a population of about 70,000, many of whom had jobs which were heavily dependant on ship building and trade in and out of Aberdeen harbour.

The renowned Aberdeen photographic pioneer George Washington Wilson captured everyday street scenes in and around the city. This included some fascinating detail of the people who were around during James' early life. Three poor young children in this 1875 image are barefooted, which would have been normal during this period.

Mercat Cross Aberdeen, MS 3792/A3109 (AUL)

Detail From Above Image

The rapidly expanding city saw the construction of many magnificent granite buildings, which Aberdeen was renowned for. James would have been 16 when the municipal buildings were completed in 1874.

MUNICIPAL BUILDINGS ABERDEEN, MS 3792/E1567 (AUL)

Despite these magnificent buildings, and increasing wealth in the city, poverty was still prevalent, as can be seen by the crowds in the weekly “Rag Fair”, at the Castle Gate.

"FRIDAY RAG FAIR", CASTLE STREET, ABERDEEN, MS 3792/B0645 (AUL)

For the poor, the sick, and the elderly who could no longer work, they were offered basic accommodation in one of Aberdeens Poorhouses. These were a slight improvement to the Workhouse of the early 1800s, and were in keeping with strict Victorian standards.

One family story mentioned that while James was on one of his long voyages, his mother became ill and his wife placed her in the St Nicholas Poorhouse. On his return home he was seemingly very upset about this, and took his mother back to the family home.

Many of the pristine granite homes built in the expanding west-end of the city, belonged to the wealthy merchants profiting from the lucrative shipping trade, granite industry, and shipbuilding.

Great Western Road MS 3792/F2021(AUL)

Aberdeen Beach MS 3792/F3745 (AUL)

One particular building, The Marischal College completed in the early1900's, highlights how Aberdeen's granite industries had reached the pinnacle of their trade.

MARISCHAL COLLEGE, ABERDEEN
UoA Ref: GB 0231 MS 3792/A0316

The photographer Archie Strachan was singly responsible for preserving the forty thousand glass plate negatives, which were left after the death of George Washington Wilson. They were eventually gifted to Aberdeen University in 1954, who are now the custodians of the priceless collection.

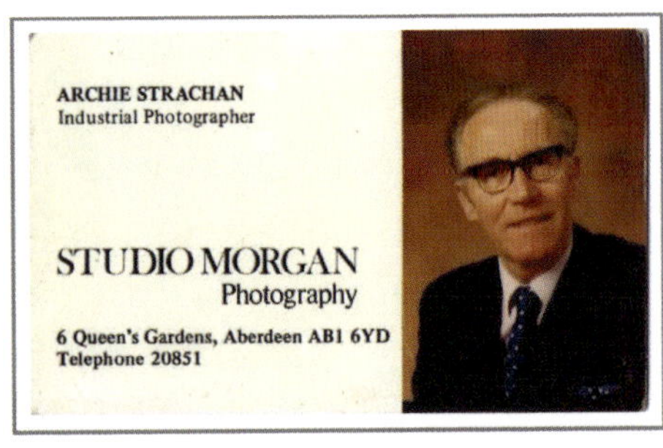

Archie Strachan stored the vast collection in tea chests in the basement of his studio for many years before a permanent home could be found for the collection at Aberdeen University.

James' Early Years

James was born on 10th August 1858, while his parents Alexander and Jane (Kerr) were living at 18 Virginia Street in Aberdeen. His father Alexander was recorded as a seaman at the time of James' birth.

1005	Mackland James	1858 August 10h am A.M. 18 Virginia Street Aberdeen	M	Alexander Mackland Seaman	Jane Mackland maiden name Kerr	Alexander Mackland father	1858 August 20th at Aberdeen [illegible] Registrar

James Mackland Birth Certificate

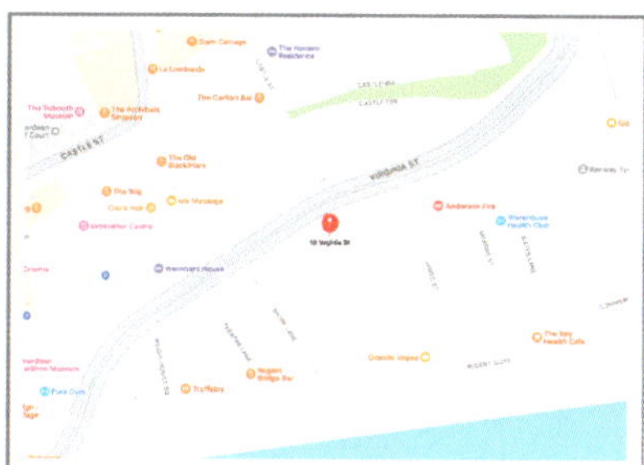

Apple Maps

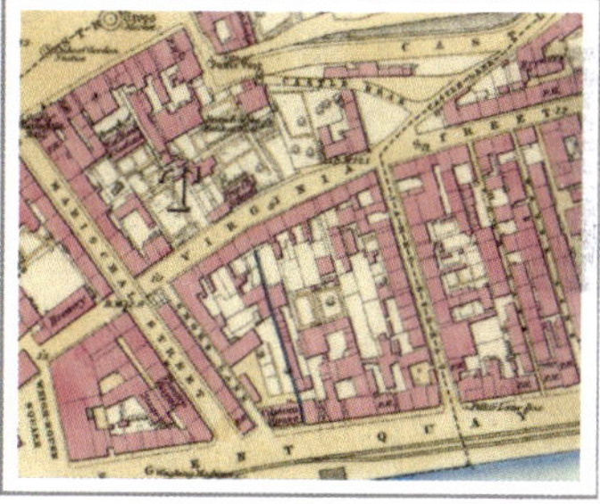

OS Maps 1864/7

Virginia Street

James was the second born of fourteen children; sadly infant mortality within his siblings was typically very high, with seven of them dying in infancy. It also appears that there were two sets of twin boys, both of whom died in the year of their birth. Three other siblings also died in the year of their birth or the following year. Twins must run in the blood line, as my grandmother Mary Ann, also had two sets of twins, sadly one of the first set died soon after birth, the other William survived. My mother Christina and her sister Willamina where the second set of twins, both of whom had a long and healthy life.

Given how small Aberdeen was in the mid-nineteenth century, James like many others, lived all of his life within half a mile of where he was born at 18 Virginia Street. The original building has long since been demolished to make way for a large warehouse complex which was occupied by the Shore Porters Society for many years. The Shore Porters Society, was established in 1498 as a semi-public body under the control of Aberdeen Town Council.

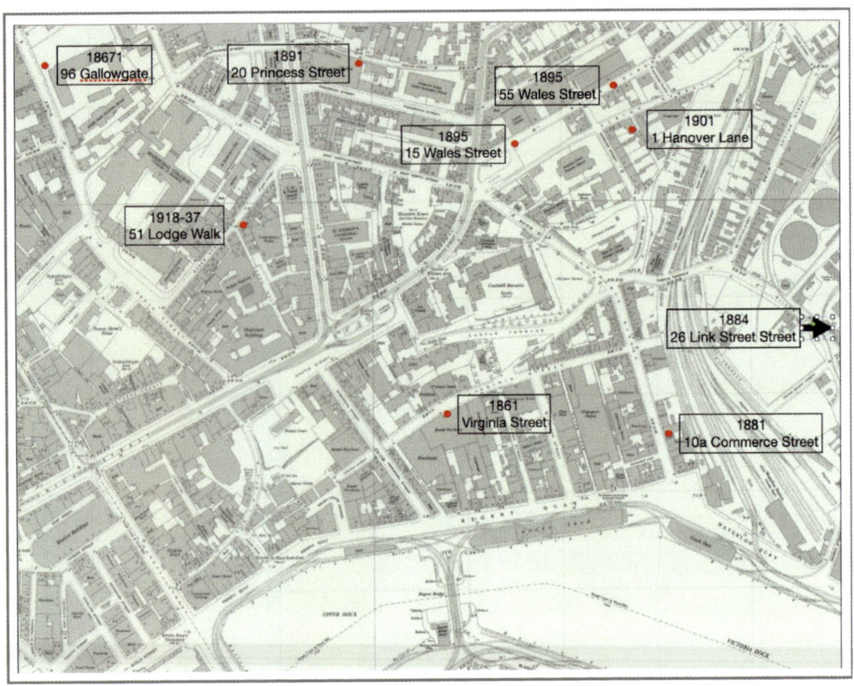

Residences

Locations:

1858 Birth	18 Virginia Street (Birth Certificate)
1861 Age 2	18 Virginia Street (Census)
1871 Age 12	96 Gallowgate (Census)
1881 Age 22	10a Commerce Street (Census)
1884 Age 25	26 Links Street (Marriage Certificate)
1886 Age 27	8 Links Street (son William's Birth Certificate)
1889 Age 30	20 Princess Street (son Alexander's Birth Certificate)
1895 Age 36	15 Wales Street
1901 Age 42	1 Hanover Lane (Census)
1911 Age 52.	55 Wales Street (Census)
1918-1937	51 Lodge Walk (1918 Mary Ann Marriage Certificate)

The 1871 census records James, age 13, living at 96 Gallowgate, his mother was listed as Head of the household, with siblings, Georgina aged 14 a millworker, Alexander age 10 and John aged 7, both scholars. Their father Alexander was not recorded in the census, as he was away from home at sea.

By the age of 13 James had already started work, he was recorded as a roper, presumably the entry level prior to starting his apprenticeship.

The Gallowgate was one of the oldest streets in Aberdeen, which lead to the execution point on Gallows Hill, which saw the demise of some poor souls at public executions. Their mortal body was left to rot for many months with just the bare bones left, before it was taken down.

The Gallowgate was similar to the well preserved buildings on Edinburgh's High Street, but sadly the shortsighted Aberdeen council decided to demolish the whole area, and build multi-storey blocks of flats.

The photo shows the approximate location of 96 Gallowgate, which was adjacent to 98, which was the entrance to Porthill Close.

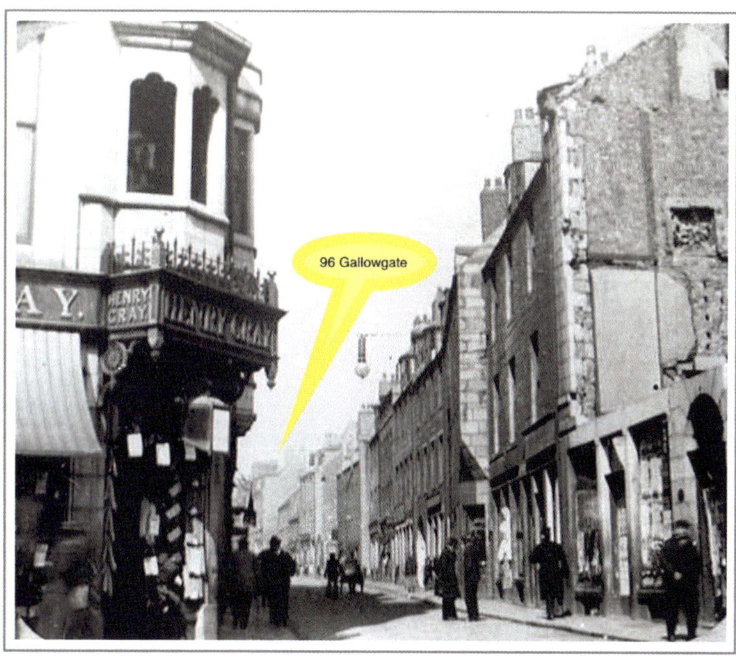

Gallowgate Looking North from the Union Building

The 1881 Census lists the family living at 10a Commerce Street, with James' mother Jane age 45, again listed as Head of the family. Siblings, John 18, Margaret 15, Mary 9, Jane 5 were recorded along with James now age 22. He was listed as "Rope and Sail Maker Apprentice".

His father Alexander had died on the 22nd January the previous year (1880), in the Royal Infirmary in Aberdeen, from "tubercular consumption of the lungs", Tuberculosis. There must have been some uncertainty around his death as a postmortem was carried out and a report was submitted to the Procurator Fiscal, to correct the original cause of death listed in his Death Certificate.

Register of Corrected Entries

for the District of St. Nicholas.

in the Burgh of Aberdeen.

The following Report of result of a Precognition has been received touching the Death of Alexander Machland Registered under No. 85 in the Register Book of Deaths for the year 1880.-

Name Age & Sex,	When & Where Died,	Cause of Death.
Alexander Mauchland - 45 years - Male -	At 11. of 22: January 1880. In the Royal Infirmary Aberdeen	Tubercular Consumption of the Lungs with weakened action of the heart combined with recent acute inflammation of the right pleural cavity. Dr. James Rodger, Aberdeen made a P.M. examination of body. (Signed) Geo. Cadenhead Procurator-Fiscal

City Procurator-Fiscal's office Aberdeen 12: February 1880

February 20th 1880, at Aberdeen

Charles Strondel, Assistant Registrar.

John Watt Registrar

July 1st 1881

Apprenticeship Age 13 to 22

Sails on clipper ships were generally made of Hemp, as it was three time stronger than Jute, and importantly it was not affected by salt water.

Sailmakers

The art of sailmaking was complex, requiring a level of expertise that took many years to acquire. The production of these massive sails, required for the new breed of heavy iron clippers, took great effort and teamwork to complete a sail that would withstand the punishment of a round the world voyage.

Sail Corner Detail

Marriage

After completing his apprenticeship and his first two voyages on The Brilliant, the next milestone in James' life was his marriage to Agnes Robertson on 13th May 1884. At this time James was living at 26 Link Street, and Agnes at number 18. Agnes was recorded as a flax mill worker, and James as rope and sailmaker journeyman.

Form 1861-1921.

EXTRACT OF AN ENTRY IN A REGISTER OF MARRIAGES, kept in the undermentioned PARISH or DISTRICT, in terms of 17° & 18° VICTORIÆ, Cap. 80, §§ 56 & 58.

No.	When, Where, and How Married.	Signatures of Parties. Rank or Profession, whether Single or Widowed, and Relationship (if any).	Age.	Usual Residence.	Name, Surname, and Rank or Profession of Father. Name, and Maiden Surname of Mother.	If a regular Marriage, Signatures of officiating Minister and Witnesses. If irregular, Date of Conviction, Decree of Declarator, or Sheriff's Warrant.	When and Where Registered, and Signature of Registrar.
172	1884 On the thirtieth day of May at 18 Links Street Aberdeen After Publication according to the Forms of the Established Church of Scotland	(Signed) James Makland Rope and Sailmaker (Journeyman) (Bachelor)	25	26 Links Street Aberdeen	Alexander Makland Seaman (Merchant Service) (deceased) Jane Makland M.S. Kerr	SIGNED Herbert Bell Minister of John Knox's Parish.	1884 June 2nd at ABERDEEN
		(Signed) Agnes Robertson Flax mill worker (Spinster)	19	18 Links Street Aberdeen	James Robertson Ship Carpenter (Journeyman) Agnes Robertson M.S. Clark	(Signed) Wm Cameron witness James Robertson witness	SIGNED Charles Stronach REGISTRAR

EXTRACTED from the REGISTER BOOK OF MARRIAGES, for the DISTRICT of ST. NICHOLAS in the BURGH of ABERDEEN, this 11th day of June 1938. Alex Benzie Asst. Registrar.

At that time Links Street was adjacent to a large rope works which stretched the length of Link Street. Most probably George & William Davidson, Merchants, Rope & Twine Manufacturers & Salmon Fishing Lessees, 35 St Clement Street. Telephone No. 355 – c.1901.

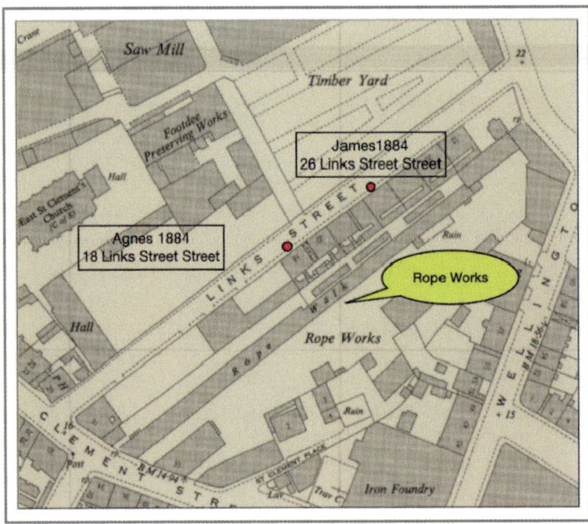

Links Street - Rope Works

Rope works were an essential part of shipbuilding, and during the mid 1800s, there were a number of them in Aberdeen, mainly around the links, due to the length of the buildings required to produce the rope. A fully rigged Clipper ship would typically require about 30 miles of rope. (reference Doric Columns).

Aberdeen Shipbuilding in the mid 1800s

By the mid 1800's there was a thriving, internationally renowned, ship building industry in Aberdeen. The shipbuilding yards supported many ancillary industries including, timber yards, saw mills, iron foundries, blacksmiths, carpenters, and importantly for James, the rope and sail making works where he served his apprenticeship.

Aberdeen Harbour 1872
Virginia Street in the foreground
Photo Courtesy of Strachan Family

At the peak of the sailing ship construction, the city supported a number of rope and sail works, many built close to the shipyards in Footdee. For example the Footdee Rope Works on Queens Links, built in 1852, was less than hundred yards from the Walter Hood and Duthie ship yards.

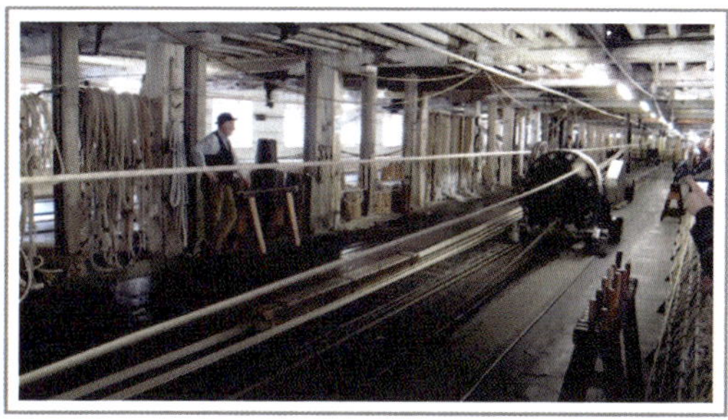

Ships from Aberdeen sailed regularly to northern Europe, the Far East, Australia, New Zealand, United States, and Canada. Many of the imports to Aberdeen were of raw materials needed for local industries, such as timber, cotton, flax, Jute, wool and coal. The exports included finished woollen, linen, and cotton goods, as well as fish, particularly herring from the trawling fleet, and salmon from the rivers Dee and Don.

As can be seen from the George Washington Willson photo, Aberdeen was a thriving port with the world famous shipyards, Duthie, and Hood.

Aberdeen Harbour
George Washington Wilson
National Galleries Scotland

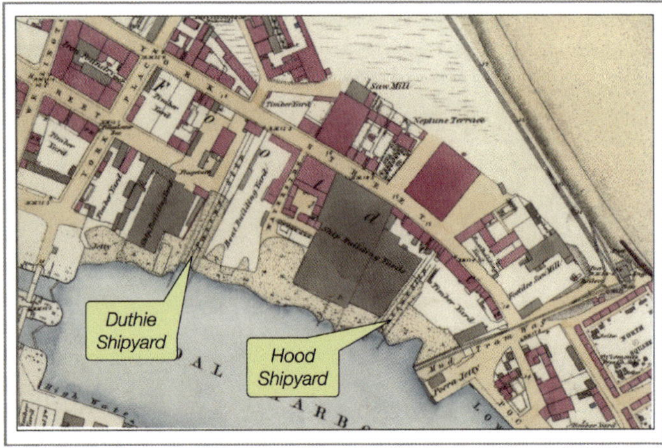

The Thermopylae is probably the best known Aberdeen built clipper ship, she was designed by Bernard Waymouth of London and built in 1867 by Walter Hood & Co. for the Aberdeen White Star Line.

Thermopylae - Dawn Departure From Foochow
Painting by Montague Dawson

The owner of the shipping line, George Thompson, wanted a clipper ship to outstrip the competition. He commissioned the Thermopylae with her iron framework supporting a wooden hull, she was built primarily for speed. Launched in 1868 she completed her maiden voyage from Gravesend to Melbourne in a record-breaking 63 days. Between 1869 and 1882 she was employed as a tea clipper plying the Far Eastern Tea Trade, where speed was of the essence bringing tea to Europe as quickly as possible. The Thermopylae and the Aberdeen Line fleet in general maintained a reputation across all their routes for style and class in their glistening green livery.

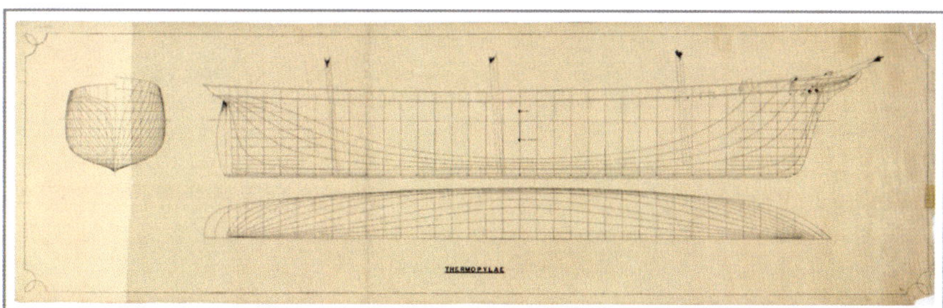

The Thermopylae had a distinctive appearance both in and out of the water, like other White Star ships she was painted in a unique green paint, which was specially produced in Aberdeen for the company. Out of the water the gleaming copper clad underside lowered the friction giving the ship additional speed.

Thermopylae
Aberdeen Maritime Museum

In 1879, before her second wool voyage from Australia, the Sydney Morning Herald eulogised about the Thermopylae:

'The fastest and handsomest ship in the world is now lying at the Circular Quay loading for London, and those who take pleasure in seeing a rare specimen of naval architecture should avail themselves of the opportunity of doing so. Of course, we allude to the Thermopylae, the celebrated Aberdeen clipper. The Thermopylae has all the appearance of a yacht, and yet she carries a good cargo, is a beautiful sea boat, and stands up to her canvas well.'

The Brilliant (Ship Number 77437)

The first ship James served on for foreign merchant service in 1881, was The Brilliant which was one of the large iron hulled sailing ships, known as "windjammers". These were seen as the ultimate evolution of the clipper ships, designed to cost effectively transport large cargos, at high speed.

The Brilliant
Artist Montague Dawson

The Brilliant was built in Aberdeen at the John Duthie Sons & Co. shipyard in Footdee, for use on the lucrative Australian trade route. It was the third ship named Brilliant built at the yard. It achieved impressively fast trips to Australia for many years, under the command of Captain Davidson.

The Duthie's were both ship builders and astute ship owners. The Duthie family had a long history of shipbuilding in Aberdeen, through several generations. A descendant of the Aberdeen family, J.F. Duthie, even started his own shipyard in Seattle, in the USA, in 1911.

Clipper ship Prince Alfred at the William Duthie Shipyard

The Brilliant's impressive dimensions were, length 254' 8" x breadth 39' 7" x depth 24' 2", and had a gross weight of 1,668 tons, with limited passenger accommodation for 1st and 2nd class passengers. There was a deck-house between the fore and main masts, and a polished teak saloon and cabin for 1st class passengers to the aft. The lower masts and yard arms were made of iron.

The Brilliant was launched at 13:10 hrs on 16th July 1877, by Miss Ann Duthie, the daughter of Mr Robert Duthie. Another famous Aberdeen clipper ship, the Pericles, was launched ten minutes earlier on the same tide from the neighbouring Walter Hood shipyard.

The Pericles and The Brilliant were to become rivals on the Australian wool trade route, racing each other to be first back to the market in London. It was a rivalry comparable to that between the Thermopylae and the Cutty Sark, when they were on the great tea races.

By all accounts the appearance of the Brilliant lived up to her name, for she had a highly polished brass rail that ran round the ship and polished teak with beautiful filigree fretwork in the panels inside the bulwarks, and a 3/4 female figurehead.

The Brilliant kept good company on the Australia run, alongside some of the fastest ships of the day, as can be seen in the photograph at Sydney harbour, berthed alongside the smaller Cutty Sark.

Circular Quay Sydney in the 1880's
(from left) the ships Yallaroi, Cutty Sark and Brilliant
State Library of South Australia PRG1373/32/68

In 1878 Brilliant made a fast passage from Sydney to London in 88 days, as a comparison the Cutty Sark did Sydney to London in 86 days in 1888/9, the Cutty Sark's record stood at 73 days for this route.

This image shows the Aberdeen built ships Brilliant and Thermopylae anchored in Sydney harbour, iron hulled Brilliant (left), at 1666 tons, and the wooden composite ship Thermopylae (right), at 949 tons. The size difference shows how much progress had been made in the construction of Aberdeen clippers ships.

Brilliant and Thermopylae anchored in Sydney Harbour
State Library of South Australia PRG1373/23/31

Brilliant Under Sail
State Library of South Australia PRG1373/3/11

First Voyage on Brilliant

As was normal before each voyage, the Brilliant had to be inspected by Lloyds to be given seaworthy certification for insurance purposes. The Brilliant was inspected in London on 18th June 1881, and given the highest insurance classification of "100-A-1".

Lloyd's Register Foundation, Report of Survey for Repairs for Brilliant 1881

REPORT of SURVEY for REPAIRS, &c.

No. in Reg. Book 731. Survey held at London. Date, first Survey 25th May. Last Survey 18th June 1881.

on the Iron S. "Brilliant". Master C. W. Davidson.

Tonnage 1488. Built at Aberdeen. When built 1877. Owners J. Duthie Sons & Co. Port belonging to Aberdeen.

Gross Tonnage 1666. Register Tonnage 1613. By whom built Duthie. Destined Voyage Sydney.

If Surveyed Afloat or in Dry Dock: Commercial dry Dk & afloat. Classed 100A1.

Last Survey, No. Port London.

REPAIRS, OR EXAMINATION AS PER RULE: SS No 1

Ceiling lifted equal to 4 strakes all fore and aft on both sides. Cement, floors &c examined and found in good condition. Spars also examined - bottom painted.

Present Condition of the Decks: Good. Rivets: Good. Windlass and Capstan: Good. Pumps: 2 No. Boats: 5 No. Condition, how ascertained: by exam. Sails: Good. Anchors No. of 3 B. 1 S. + 2 K. Cables: Good. Cement, When put on 1877. Hawsers and Warps: 5 No. Caulking of Bottom, Deck, & Waterways: Good. Scuppers: Good. Cargo and Main Hatchways: Good. Hatches: Good.

General Observations, Opinion as to Class, &c.

She is now in good condition and in my opinion eligible to continue as classed and marked SS. Lon No 1. 81

Will. C. Davies, Surveyor to Lloyd's Register of British and Foreign Shipping

The Amount of Entry Fee ... Special ... £4 : 4 : – received by me, 18th June 1881

Certificate (if required) to be sent as per margin ... 5/-

Committee's Minute: Friday, June 24th 1881

Character assigned: 100 A 1

James signed the crew agreement on 30th June 1881, after the Brilliant started loading in London on 10th June 1881. James as the sailmaker formed a key part of the core skilled crew, along with the ships master, first and second mates, carpenter, boatswain, and importantly the cook.

The crew were contracted to be onboard the ship by noon on Saturday 2nd July. Press reports show that the Brilliant departed London on 7th July, with a cargo for the Houlder Brothers & Company, on a voyage to Sydney which took 88 days.

Agreement and Account of Crew

For anyone to be engaged for a voyage on a foreign going ship, they had to sign a formal agreement with the company, called the "Agreement and Account of Crew", which defined their remuneration, obligations, and the details of the voyage. After an extensive search I managed to locate the crew agreements for each of James' voyages.

These were located in the Maritime History Archive, of the Memorial University of Newfoundland, where all the original documents are now stored.

The Merchant Shipping Act of 1835 introduced the requirement for the master of every large foreign going ship to enter into an agreement with each member of his crew detailing the conditions of their employment, including rates of pay as well as penalties to pay in the event of breaking any of the terms of the contract. These agreements, are commonly referred to as Ship's Articles.

The first page of the Agreement and Account of Crew records the name of the ship as well as its official number, and port of registry (Aberdeen). It then records the name and address of the registered managing owner (John Duthie, York Place, Aberdeen), and the number of seamen for whom accommodation is certified, in this case it is fifty.

James contracted for a voyage of up to two years, and apart from having Sydney as their destination, the crew agreement also stipulated that the ship could stop at any other port in Australia, India, China, the Pacific, and Atlantic oceans. Their return port could be anywhere in the United Kingdom.

We can assume that James had made the arrangements to join the ship through the John Duthie office in Aberdeen, before setting off with his working tools and enough belongings to last him two years. His trip to London to join the Brilliant, would probably have been by rail, but could also have been by sea in a Duthie vessel, as it was still a regular trade route to London.

Brilliant Agreement and Account of Crew

AGREEMENT No.58903

AGREEMENT AND ACCOUNT OF CREW.

(FOREIGN-GOING SHIP.)

EXECUTED IN TWENTY PAGES.

Name of Ship.	Official No.	Port of Registry.	Port No. and Date of Register.	Registered Tonnage. Gross.	Net.
"Brilliant"	77437	Aberdeen	9/1877	1665	1613

REGISTERED MANAGING OWNER. Name.	Address.	No. of Seamen for whom accommodation is certified.	Distance in feet and inches between centre of Maximum load line disc and upper edge of line indicating the position of the First Deck above it.
John Duthie	York Place, Aberdeen	50	4.6

The several Persons whose names are hereto subscribed, and whose descriptions are contained on the other side or sides, and of whom Fourteen are engaged as Sailors, hereby agree to serve on board the said Ship, in the several capacities expressed against their respective Names, on a Voyage from London to Sydney and any port or ports in Australia, India, China, Pacific or Atlantic Oceans, West Indies or America, trading backwards and forwards until her return to a final port of discharge in the United Kingdom. Voyage not to exceed two years.

SUBSTITUTES.

Equivalent at the Master's option.

And the Crew agree to conduct themselves in an orderly, faithful, honest, and sober manner, and to be at all times diligent in their respective Duties, and to be obedient to the lawful Commands of the said Master, or of any Person who shall lawfully succeed him, and of their Superior Officers, in every thing relating to the said Ship and the Stores and Cargo thereof, whether on board, in boats, or on shore: in consideration of which Services to be duly performed, the said Master hereby agrees to pay to the said Crew as Wages the Sums against their Names respectively expressed, and to supply them with Provisions according to the above Scale: And it is hereby agreed, That any Embezzlement or wilful or negligent Destruction of any part of the Ship's Cargo or Stores shall be made good to the Owner out of the Wages of the Person guilty of the same: And if any Person enters himself as qualified for a duty which he proves incompetent to perform, his Wages shall be reduced in proportion to his incompetency: And it is also agreed, That the Regulations authorised by the Board of Trade, which are printed herein, and numbered 1 to 12 inclusive, are adopted by the parties hereto, and shall be considered as embodied in this Agreement: And it is also agreed, That if any Member of the Crew considers himself to be aggrieved by any breach of the Agreement or otherwise, he shall represent the same to the Master or Officer in charge of the Ship in a quiet and orderly manner, who shall thereupon take such steps as the case may require: And it is also agreed, That No money advanced abroad. Wearing a Knife without a Laniard forfeit two days pay. Any man not joining the Ship at the appointed time substitute will be engaged.

The authority of the Owner or Agent for the allotments mentioned within is in my possession.

In Witness whereof the said parties have subscribed their Names on the other Side or Sides hereof on the days against their respective Signatures mentioned.

Signed by [signature] Master, on the 20th day of June 1881.

Date of Commencement of Voyage.	Port at which Voyage commenced.	Date of Termination of Voyage.	Port at which Voyage terminated.	Date of Delivery of Lists to Superintendent.	I hereby declare to the truth of the Entries in this Agreement and Account of Crew, &c.
20/6/81	London	17/8/82	London	18/8/82	[signature] Master.

[Twenty Pages.]

Additional details on the front page, stipulate that no advance of wages will be made abroad, presumably to discourage crew members deserting ship in port. There is also a fine of two days wages for bearing a knife without a laniard, probably to prevent it being dropped when attending to the sails.

The second page of the agreement contains the signature of each crew member as well as personal details including place of birth, and their position in the crew. It was interesting to actually see James' very neat signature on the form, verifying his engagement in the crew, and confirming that this was his first ship on foreign service.

PARTICULARS OF ENGAGEMENT.

Reference No.	SIGNATURES OF CREW. 1	Age. 2	Town or County where born. 3	If in the Reserve, No. of Commission or R.V.R. 4	Ship in which he last served. State Name, and Official No. or Port she belonged to. 5	Year. 6	Date and Place of joining this Ship. Date. 7	Place. 8	In what Capacity engaged, and if Master, Mate, or Engineer, No. of his Certificate. 9	Time at which he is to be on board. 10
1	[illegible] (Master to sign first.)	1847	Edinburgh		Brilliant	188[illegible]			87.214 Master	
2	John Leitch	1850	Glasgow		do				1st Mate 01494	
3	[illegible] F. W. Fox	1858	Derby		Cynisca				2 Mate 082.31	
4	John Ewan	1861	Aberdeen		First Ship Allahabad				Carpenter	
5	Thomas Carter	1836	Gosport		Allahabad	1881			Bosun	
6	James Mackland	1857	Aberdeen		First Ship				Sailmaker	

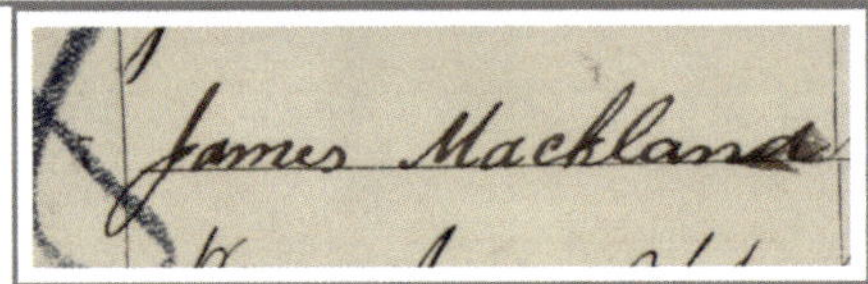

His remuneration for this trip was recorded on the third page, as £3- 5s per month, with an allotment of £1-17s-6d per month to be provided to his family at home for the duration of the voyage. Looking at the wages being paid to other crew members it is obvious that James had accepted the lower rate to secure his entry into foreign service. As a comparison of wages, one source suggests that the average wage in Scotland in the mid 1880s was just £23-6s per year, less than £2 per month.

The crew agreement showed that there ware substantial numbers of crew members being discharged and recruited at each port of call. Many of the crew leaving were by mutual agreement with the ship's master, however several were through desertion, and hospitalisation.

The master of the Brilliant was Captain Charles William Davidson who was born in Edinburgh in 1847, he served his apprenticeship in the Aberdeen sailing vessel Liberator, and having completed his time when the ship was on a voyage, was rated boatswain for the rest of it. He was promoted to second mate in 1868, as soon as he was qualified. After a voyage as third mate, he returned to the Liberator as second mate, then first mate, serving in the same capacity in the ship John Duthie until he got his master's certificate in 1874.

On arrival in Sydney, a formal listing of the crew was made showing that the Brilliant arrived on the 3rd October 1881.

The listing shows that there was a crew of 35, including 5 apprentices, and 2 sixteen year olds listed as "Boy". There were only 2 passengers on this trip, and incredibly 5 stowaways, who don't appear in the crew agreement.

The crew, as in most of these voyages, seem to have been gathered from all over the UK and Europe, no doubt many of them were looking for a one way trip so that they could start a new life in Australia.

Eighteen of the crew were discharged in Sydney on the understanding that they forfeited their wages, with the exception of the Swedish crew members, T. Peter Peterson, and Charles Brown who were left behind having been admitted to hospital.

Fifteen new crew members were engaged in Sydney for the next leg of their voyage to Newcastle.

Crew List for The Brilliant Arrival in Sydney on 3rd October 1881

INWARD.

A LIST of the Crew and Passengers arrived in the Ship Brilliant of ... Master, Burthen 1613 Tons, from the Port of London to Sydney, New South Wales, 3 October 1881.

Seamen's Names.	Station.	Age.	Of what Nation.	Names of Passengers.	Description.	Remarks.

Transcript of Crew List

BRILLIANT

OF ABERDEEN, CHARLES WILLIAM DAVIDSON, MASTER, BURTHEN 1613 TONS
FROM THE PORT OF LONDONTO SYDNEY, NEW SOUTH WALES, 3rd OCTOBER, 1881

Surname	Given name	Station	Age	Of what Nation	Status	Comments
DAVIDSON	CHARLES WILLIAM	CAPTAIN			CREW	
LEITCH	JOHN	MATE	1855	GLASGOW	CREW	
FOX	ERNEST T.W.	2nd MATE	1858	DERBY	CREW	
GAVIN	JOHN	CARPENTER	1861	ABERDEEN	CREW	
CARTER	THOMAS	BOATSWAIN	1836	GOSPORT	CREW	
MACHLAN	JAMES	SAILMAKER	1859	ABERDEEN	CREW	
APPS	HENRY JAS.	STEWARD	1840	WORCESTER	CREW	
McCAFFREY	JOHN H.	COOK	1845	DUNDEE	CREW	
BLAIR	JOHN	A. B.	1859	MAYFAIR	CREW	
GREENWAY	FREDERICK	A. B.	1860	FALSMOUTH	CREW	
MELVILLE	JOHN	A. B.	1840	LIVERPOOL	CREW	
HENDERSON	JAMES	A. B.	1836	SHETLAND	CREW	
TAYLOR	JOHN	A. B.	1853	DEVON	CREW	
PESTWAN	ROGER	A. B.	1862	CHELMSFORD	CREW	
QUETY	WILLIAM	A. B.	1841	QUEBEC	CREW	
WALSH	WILLIAM	A. B.	1860	DUBLIN	CREW	
SEYMOUR	JOSEPH	A. B.	1839	DUBLIN	CREW	
ALGAR	RICHARD	A. B.	1857	LONDON	CREW	
BLACKWELL	THOMAS	A. B.	1853	LONDON	CREW	
KEENAN	PETER	A. B.	1853	DUBLIN	CREW	
RUCHAN	JAMES	A. B.	1832	LONDON	CREW	
WHELITORN	THOMAS	A. B.	1858	LONDON	CREW	
JOHNSON	FREDERICK	A. B.	1853	FINLAND	CREW	
PETERSON	T. PETER	A. B.	1834	SWEDEN	CREW	
SHEHAN	MICHAEL	BOY	1865	SNOWDON	CREW	
UPLEST	THOMAS	BOY	1865	SNOWDON	CREW	
BROWN	CHARLES	A. B.	1840	SWEDEN	CREW	
PAGE	GEORGE	A. B.	28	DOVER	CREW	
JAMIESON	FREDERICK	O. S.	17	KIRKEALDY	CREW	
STEWART	JAMES	ASST. STEWARD	16	LONDON	CREW	
FOREMAN	ROBERT WILLIAM	APPRENTICE	1862	LONDON	CREW	
FLOWER	GEORGE ALEXANDER	APPRENTICE	1856	LONDON	CREW	
MANUS	THOMAS LEWIS	APPRENTICE	1864	LONDON	CREW	
BANYARD	ROBERT JAMES	APPRENTICE	1865	LONDON	CREW	
COX	W.C.	APPRENTICE	1866	LONDON	CREW	
PHIPPS	SAMUEL	UPHOLSTERER			PASSENGER	
ROSS	WILLIAM HENRY				PASSENGER	
BYRNE	AMBROSE				STOWAWAY	
GALLAGHER	JOHN WILLIAM				STOWAWAY	
McKNIGHT	JOHN				STOWAWAY	
WAKEFIELD	ALFRED				STOWAWAY	Lic. 24/10/81
PEARSON	JOSEPH				STOWAWAY	

After unloading at Sydney the Brilliant picked up a cargo of wool bales in New Zealand for their return trip to London, but first they sailed about 80 miles North to Newcastle in New South Wales, possibly to load a cargo of coal, or ballast for the return trip round Cape Horn.

Brilliant at anchor in Sydney Harbour about 1880
State Library of South Australia PRG1373/3/12

They arrived in the busy port of Newcastle on 14th February 1882. On this leg of the voyage, sadly one of the young boys in the crew fell from the main mast suffering serious injuries, he was taken to hospital on arrival in Newcastle. He must have been reunited with the ship before they departed, as he was recorded in the crew agreement as being discharged from the ship in London on their return home.

INTERCOLONIAL TELEGRAMS.

(REUTER'S TELEGRAMS.)

NEW SOUTH WALES.

SYDNEY, Saturday.

The King of Italy has conferred on Sir Henry Parkes, through the Italian consul, the order of Knight Commander of the Crown of Italy. Mr Wise, the emigration agent, and Mr Marsh, stipendiary magistrate, have been named Companions of the order, in recognition of their kindness to the Italians belonging to the Marquis de Ray's expedition.

A boy fell to-day from the mainmast of the ship Brilliant, and was taken to the hospital. His condition is serious.

The busy port of Newcastle at the mouth of the Hunter River, was famous for shipping coal from their productive coal mines which had been in operation since the 1790s.

Newcastle Harbour from Fort Scratchley

Ships also loaded ballast for their homeward journey to the UK, in preparation for the notoriously dangerous stormy transit around Cape Horn.

Port of Newcastle Ballast Loading
Newcastle University's Cultural Collections

On arrival in Newcastle there was another radical change of crew, with ten sailors being discharged with mutual consent this time, and paid £1-13s wages. The crew was supplemented with fourteen new members.

There seems to have been a change of shipping agents for the return voyage, with Dangar, Gedye, and Company listed as the shipping agent. This was a partnership between Charles Townsend Gedye originally from Devonport, and Frederick Holkham Dangar an Australian citizen; their successful partnership in the Sydney-London trade lasted until it was sold in 1889.

After loading at Newcastle the Brilliant set sail for Port Lyttelton (Christchurch) in South Island, New Zealand, to load cargo for their return voyage to London.

The Brilliant arrived in Port Lyttelton on what appears to have been a bright autumn day on 22nd March 1882, after leaving Newcastle.

PORT OF LYTTELTON.

WEATHER REPORT—March 22.

9 a.m.—Weather, blue sky. Wind, calm. Barometer, 30.03; thermometer, 58.

High Water—This Day.

Morning, 6.35; evening, 7.3.

ARRIVED—March 21.

Tui, s.s., 55 tons, Pope, from Wellington via Kaikoura. Passengers — Messrs Warsden, Clarke, Larsen, Coil, Jacobson, Ryan, Rossiter. Cuff and Graham, agents.

March 22.

Hawea, s.s., 462 tons, Kennedy, from Port Chalmers via Akaroa. Passengers—Mesdames Hayes and two children, Meech, Wells and four children, Mr and Mrs Morice, Captain Sinclair, Messrs Moore, Dalglish, Fueston, Roby, Anderson. Steerage, 2. Union Steamship Company, agents.

Brilliant, ship, 1613 tons, Davidson, from Newcastle. N.Z. Shipping Co., agents.

This panoramic image, of Lyttelton harbour, was taken from the Corsair Bay road on 24th March 1882, when there were no fewer than twenty-four overseas sailing vessels in the inner harbour. The image is from the State Library of South Australia's photographic collection, with what appears to be the Brilliant mid-harbour. James would have been on the ship at the time the photograph was taken, on his return voyage on the Brilliant, on his way back to London.

Brilliant at Port Lyttelton 1882
State Library of South Australia

Detail of the Brilliant in the Panoramic Image
State Library of South Australia

On arrival in Port Lyttelton, six members of the crew were discharged, and another two seamen deserted the ship. Before departing eleven new crew members were signed up for the trip to London.

Their short time in Port Lyttelton wasn't without incident, the first involved some heated differences between the new cook Daniel Davis, and the chief officer. The confrontation was reported on 1st April in the Port of Lyttelton press. Daniel had joined the ship in Newcastle, on a rather substantial wage of £6 per month.

DAMAGE AND ASSAULT.—The cook belonging to the ship Brilliant, Daniel Davis, was charged with assaulting the chief officer of the ship. He admitted the offence, and was further charged with damaging the ship's property by destroying some fat and marking the ship's decks. The damage was estimated at 33s. The Bench sentenced the prisoner to twenty-four hours' imprisonment, and to pay the damage.

The second incident in the same press article involved the seaman Alfred Spencer a 35 year old Londoner who also joined the ship in Newcastle, he was reported absent without leave, and sent back to the ship to fulfil his contract of employment. He was discharged in London with £17-2s-1d.

ABSENT WITHOUT LEAVE.—A. Spencer, charged with being absent from the ship Brilliant, was cautioned and sent back to his ship.

Another, more serious court incident involved Fredrick Hob, who had signed on in Lyttelton as an able bodied seaman, for The Brilliant's return voyage to London. He was arrested for alleged desertion of his wife Selina. He did not rejoin the ship, and was struck off the crew agreement.

ALLEGED WIFE DESERTION.—Fred Hobden, who had been arrested on board of the ship Brilliant, on which he had shipped as A.B. for a voyage to England, was charged with intending to desert his wife Selina. He stated that a deed of separation between the parties had been executed four years ago, and obtained a remand till Monday, May 15th, for its production.

After arriving in Australia in 3rd October 1881, the Brilliant eventually set sail for London from Port Lyttelton on 13th May 1882, under the New Zealand Shipping Company, as agents.

Details of the ships cargo listed after clearing customs formalities were published in the Lyttleton Times on 13th May.

The cargo was for multiple shippers, and included 1455 bales of wool, 50 pockets of wool, 213 bales of flax, 606 cases of gum, 28 packets of gum, 3 cases rabbit skins, 3 cases shells, 10 cases of cheese, 14 cases of honey, 2 kegs honey, 11793 sacks of wheat, 200 sacks of chicory, 1815 sacks of beans, and 7 packages of sundry items.

Brilliant: 1455 bales wool, 50 pockets do, 213 bales flax, 606 cases gum, 28 pkgs do, 3 cases rabbit skins, 3 do shells, 10 do cheese, 14 do honey, 2 kegs do, 11,793 sacks wheat, 200 sacks chicory, 1815 sacks beans, 7 pkgs sundries. Shippers—Lewis and Gould; Ulrich; Desborough; Miles and Co.; N.Z Loan and Mercantile Agency Co.; Campbell Bros.; N.Z. Farmers' Co-operative Association; G. A. Anstey; J. M. Heywood and Co.; R. Wilkin and Co.; Cuff and Graham; Wood, Sinclair and Co.; Chrystall and Co.; A. Moore and Co.; M. Mitchell and Co.; J. Murgatroyd; J. and J. Tinline; R. Paflett; T. Cawthorne; W. B. Jackson.

The ship Brilliant cleared at the Customs for London yesterday, with a full cargo of produce and two passengers.

Cargo List For Brilliant Return Voyage

After a voyage of 96 days the Brilliant arrived back at Gravesend on 17th August 1882, and cleared customs on the18th August, with a cargo for the Holden Brothers & Co.

The photo shows in the foreground cargo barges known as “Lighters”. At the height of the port's prosperity some 6000 lighters were engaged in carrying cargoes from the docks. This remarkable photograph supports the claim of London lightermen that they were often able to walk across the docks, by jumping from the deck of one craft to another.

West India Dock, London
Royal Museums Greenwich

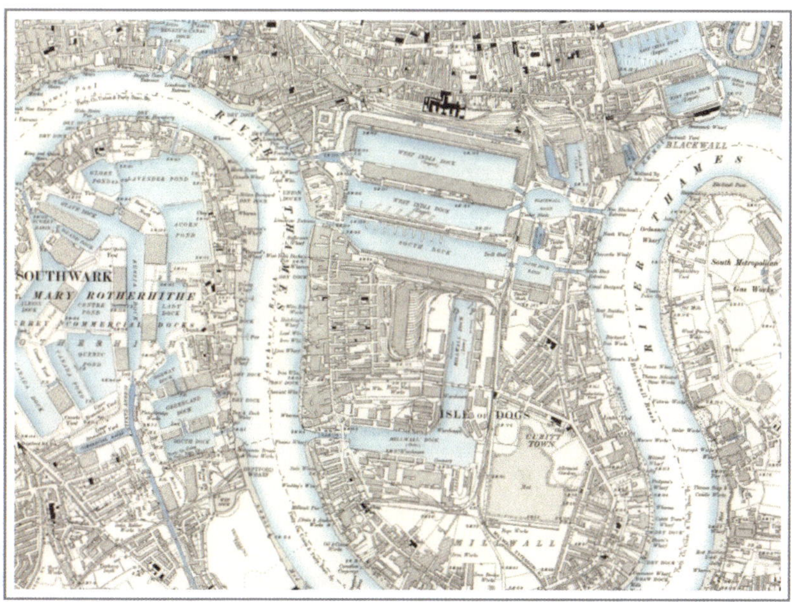

West India Docks (OS Maps1899)

Second Voyage on Brilliant

James was contracted for a second voyage on the Brilliant from 4th October 1882, after what seems like a very short shore leave. The ship started loading on 17th August 1882, again with a cargo for the Houlder Brothers & Co.

PASSAGE TO SYDNEY.—The Splendid Aberdeen-built CLIPPER SHIP "BRILLIANT," 1613 Tons Reg., 100 A1, owned by Messrs John Duthie, Sons, & Co., of Aberdeen, and commanded by Captain C. W. DAVIDSON, to leave about 20th AUGUST, has excellent accommodation for first-class passengers. Exceptional advantages are offered, the Saloon being fitted with One-birth Cabins, furnished with Bedding, Linen, and all requisites. First-class Apprentices are required for this vessel, as well as for the "Abergeldie," owned by the same firm, and leaving for Sydney on the 10th August. For full particulars apply to HOULDER BROTHERS & CO., 146 LEADENHALL STREET, LONDON, E.C.

Press Advert 1884

The press cutting proudly advertises the passenger accommodation for a voyage to Sydney on the Brilliant, at the princely sum of 40 guineas.

Agreement and Account of Crew

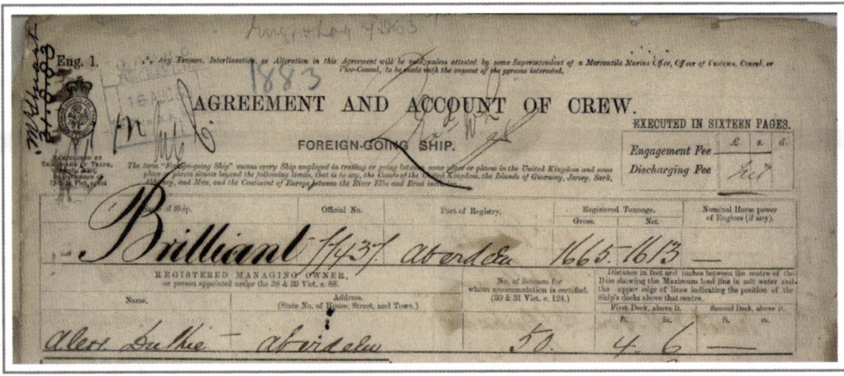

Eng. 1.

1883

AGREEMENT AND ACCOUNT OF CREW.

EXECUTED IN SIXTEEN PAGES.

FOREIGN-GOING SHIP.

Engagement Fee	£	s.	d.
Discharging Fee			

Name of Ship.	Official No.	Port of Registry.	Registered Tonnage. Gross.	Net.	Nominal Horse power of Engines (if any).
Brilliant	71437	Aberdeen	1665	1613	—

Registered Managing Owner, or person appointed under the 38 & 39 Vict. c. 88. Name.	Address. (State No. of House, Street, and Town.)	No. of Seamen for whom accommodation is certified. (30 & 31 Vict. c. 124.)	First Deck, above it. ft.	in.	Second Deck, above it. ft.	in.
Alext Duthie	Aberdeen	50.	4	6	—	

For the second trip on the Brilliant, again with the ship's master Captain Davidson. The registered owner for this voyage was Alexander Duthie. The voyage to Sydney, was for up to two years, but this time the return port could be anywhere in the UK, or Continental Europe.

This could have made his return home to Aberdeen expensive and quite challenging; luckily James was discharged back in London.

The crew were contracted to join the ship by 6am on 7th October 1882, which only gave James about six weeks at home with his family.

Having completed his first trip on the Brilliant, James had an increase in his wages to £4-10s per month, with an allotment to his family back home of £2-5s for each month he was away from home.

The crew agreement gave details of the provisions to be provided to the crew each week, and gives an insight into the tedious diet the crew were to endure for the duration of the trip, and notably no spirits were allowed.

A supply of lime and lemon juice were also to be supplied to prevent scurvy.

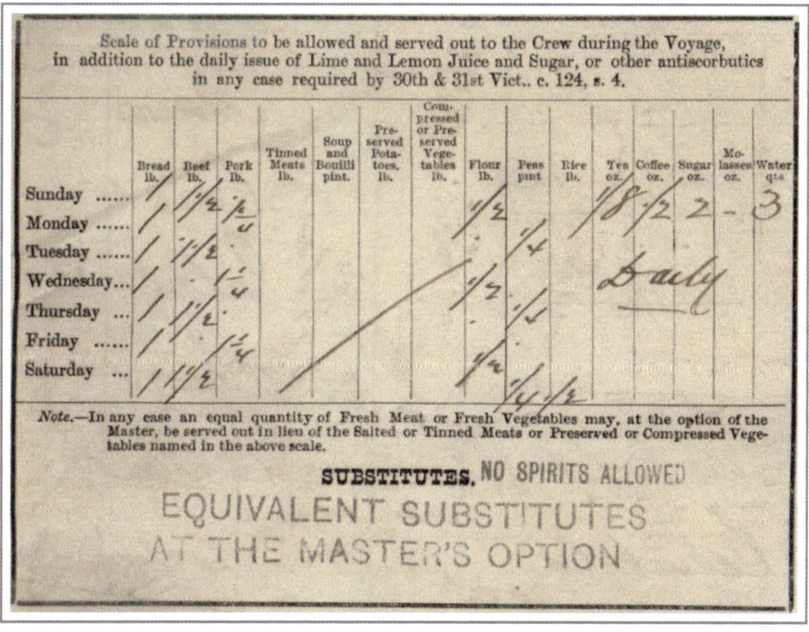

Scale of Provisions to be allowed and served out to the Crew during the Voyage, in addition to the daily issue of Lime and Lemon Juice and Sugar, or other antiscorbutics in any case required by 30th & 31st Vict.. c. 124, s. 4.

	Bread lb.	Beef lb.	Pork lb.	Tinned Meats lb.	Soup and Bouilli pint.	Preserved Potatoes. lb.	Compressed or Preserved Vegetables lb.	Flour lb.	Peas pint	Rice lb.	Tea oz.	Coffee oz.	Sugar oz.	Molasses oz.	Water qts
Sunday	1	1 1/2	1 1/4					1/2			1/8	1/2	2	-	3
Monday	1							.	1/4						
Tuesday	1	1 1/2	.												
Wednesday...	1	.	1 1/4					1/2			Daily				
Thursday ...	1	1 1/2	.					-	1/4						
Friday	1	.	1 1/4						.						
Saturday ...	1	1 1/2						1/2							

Note.—In any case an equal quantity of Fresh Meat or Fresh Vegetables may, at the option of the Master, be served out in lieu of the Salted or Tinned Meats or Preserved or Compressed Vegetables named in the above scale.

SUBSTITUTES. NO SPIRITS ALLOWED

EQUIVALENT SUBSTITUTES AT THE MASTER'S OPTION

Crew Provisions

After completing the loading of their cargo and passengers, the Brilliant cast off, and left the London docks on 7th October 1882. They were first taken under tow along the Thames by the steam tug Robert Bruce, eventually setting sails on 10th October for their long voyage to Sydney.

A location report in the Shipping and Mercantile Gazette on Saturday 28th October 1882, shows the Brilliant at 45' North 8' West, in the Bay of Biscay, on route for the Cape of Good Hope.

After a journey of 87 days dock to dock, the Brilliant arrived in Sydney's outer harbour on 30th December 1882, and completed immigration formalities on 2rd January 1883. On this voyage there was a crew of 36, again with Captain Charles Davidson in command, who on this trip was accompanied by his wife and child. This was his second wife who had the very unusual first name, Fotheringham, and their child Hilda who was born 25th August 1881. Charles and Fotheringham were married 21st Aug 1880 at All Saints church in London.

On this trip there was only one stowaway, three passengers in first class, one in second class, and one in third class.

Crew List for The Brilliant Arrival in Sydney on 2nd January 1883

INWARD.

A LIST of the Crew and Passengers arrived in the Ship Brilliant of Aberdeen, Charles William Davidson Master, Burthen 1613 Tons, from the Port of London to Sydney, New South Wales, 2 January 1883.

Seamen's Names.	Station.	Age.	Of what Nation.	Names of Passengers.	Description.	Remarks.

Transcript of Crew List

BRILLIANT

OF ABERDEEN, DAVIDSON, MASTER, BURTHEN 1613 TONS
FROM THE PORT OF LONDON TO SYDNEY, NEW SOUTH WALES, 2ND JANUARY DECEMBER 1883

Surname	**Given name**	**Station**	Y.O.B.	**Of what Nation**	**Status**	**Comments**
DAVIDSON	CHARLES WILLIAM	MASTER			CREW	
LEITCH	JOHN	1st MATE	1855	GLASGOW	CREW	
FOX	ERNEST T W	2nd MATE	1858	DERBYSHIRE ?	CREW	
FLOVER	GEORGE	3rd MATE	1857	LISBON	CREW	
CARTER	T	BOATSWAIN	1837	PORTSMOUTH	CREW	
GAVIN	JOHN	CARPENTER	1862	PORTSMOUTH	CREW	
MACKLAND	JAMES	SAILMAKER	1859	PORTSMOUTH	CREW	
APPS	HENRY J	STEWARD	1838	WORCESTER	CREW	
LEWIS	EDARO	2ND STEWARD	1862	BHAIN	CREW	
LE BARBI	TH	COOK	1843	FRANCE	CREW	
HULL	WALTER	A. B.	1859	LEICESTER	CREW	
KELLY	ANDREW	A. B.	1852	LIVERPOOL	CREW	
BJORKLAND	H	A. B.	1862	GOTHENBERG, SWEDN	CREW	
OLIVER	F	A. B.	1856	ST JOHNS	CREW	
MATHER	JOHN	A. B.	1845	WELLINGTON, NZ	CREW	
PETROVICH	D	A. B.	1854	AUSTRIA	CREW	
MITCHELL	JOHN	A. B.	1852	KIRKALDY	CREW	
RANDA	JOHN	A. B.	1860	GOTHLAND	CREW	
SMITH	WM	A. B.	1863	BOSTON	CREW	
O'FLAHERTY	B	A. B.	1843	GALWAY	CREW	
LAURENCE	JAMES	A. B.	1862	PORTSMOUTH	CREW	
COLVILL	HENRY	A. B.	1859	LONDON	CREW	
WARDEN	JOHN	A. B.	1854	JUNDLE ?	CREW	
GORDON	J	A. B.	1844	INVERNESS	CREW	
STEVENS	ABAT	A. B.	1859	LONDON	CREW	
CARTER	ARTHUR	A. B.	1860	W COWES	CREW	
OLSEN	CHAS	A. B. & QUARTER MASTER	1841	FREDERICKSTADT, NORWAY	CREW	
ADMODT	A	A. B.	1853	FRA?, NORWAY	CREW	
ASSTED ?	THOS	O. S.	1865	LONDON	CREW	
SHEHAN	MICHAEL	O. S.	1865	LONDON	CREW	
COTTAIN	WALTER	GROOM FOR HORSES	1859	ROXHIN ?	CREW	
NOR _ ?	ROBERT WILLIAM BEULE	APPRENTICE	1862	LONDON	CREW	
FOWLER	GEORGE ALEXANDER	APPRENTICE	1857	LONDON	CREW	
BANYARD	ROBERT JS	APPRENTICE	1864	LONDON	CREW	
THOMAS	THOMAS LEWIS	APPRENTICE	1863	LONDON	CREW	
GEFFARD	FREDERICK WALTER	APPRENTICE	1865	LONDON	CREW	
JAMIESON	FREDK PEAK	APPRENTICE	1864	LONDON	CREW	
DAVIDSON		MRS			PASSENGER	SALOON
DAVIDSON	CHILD				PASSENGER	SALOON
GARRETT	PAUL	MR			PASSENGER	SALOON
THOMAS	G T	MR			PASSENGER	SALOON
RYAN	J H	MR			PASSENGER	SALOON
MCADAM	WILLIAM				PASSENGER	2ND SALOON
MCADAM	ROBERT				PASSENGER	3rd SALOON
ROBSON	J				STOWAWAY	

Interestingly the crew list included an unpaid Walter Cottan, as a "Groom for Horses". The cargo on this trip included a consignment of six horses, as reported with some enthusiasm, in the Australian Town and County Journal on 13th January 1883. The horses were imported by Messers Dangar and Town. The groom was credited with taking good care of the horses during the voyage.

THE AUSTRALIAN TOWN AND COUNTRY JOURNAL

Circulation Ten Thousand Copies greater than that of any other Weekly in Australia.

VOL. XXVII.—NO. 679. SYDNEY, SATURDAY, JANUARY 13, 1883. PRICE SIXPENCE.

Good Strains of Horse Stock.

The recent importations of thoroughbred horses to our already long list is a good proof that breeders here intend keeping pace with breeders of the most excellent strains in the old country. On the present occasion Messrs. W. J. Dangar and A. Town are the importers per sailing ship Brilliant. The lot, six in number, reflect the highest credit on Walter Cottan, their custodian, whom Mr. Dangar took over with him on purpose to bring out his purchases. The first introduced to our notice at Carling's Bazaar was Multum in Parvo, a dark chestnut stallion, of the Suffolk Punch breed, a nicely rounded two-year-old, possessing great bone and substance, with short legs. There was another stallion of the same type, but lighter in colour, named Waxworks, and is very symmetrical, while in the adjoining box a Suffolk Punch filly, chestnut in colour, rather inappropriately named Dandy. She possesses plenty of length, is roomy, and low to the ground. With such animals as the above our light draught stock should be greatly improved.

Additional details of the cargo Brilliant delivered to Sydney, included 169 packages which consisted of hams, dried milk, Scotch salmon, cutlets and kippered, and game, which were destined for H.S. Bird and Co.. In addition there were 150 casks of Anglo-Bavarian ale, 5 quarter casks of brandy, 1 pipe of old port (a large barrel 350 - 500 litres), 1 butt of Amontillado sherry, and one case of pâté de foie gras, for importers Peate and Harcourt.

Ex Brilliant: 169 packages hams, D. M. milk, Scotch salmon, cutlets and kippered, game, &c.—H. S. BIRD AND CO.

Ex Ballarat: 40 cases hams, Cheddar, N. Wilts, and Edam cheese—PEATE AND HARCOURT.

Ex Brilliant: 150 casks Anglo-Bavarian ale; 5 quarter-casks brandy; 1 pipe old port; 1 butt amontillado sherry; 1 case paté de foie gras—PEATE AND HARCOURT.

Captain Davidson's detailed account of the voyage from London was reported in the Sydney Morning Herald on 25th January, reinforcing the ship being *"one of the crack ships in the trade"*. The ship lost the foresail, and the lower fore-topsail, in a storm on 10th December.

The clipper ship Brilliant, which arrived on December 31, from London, with a large and valuable general cargo, completed the passage from the Lizards in 81 days, thus sustaining the reputation she has earned for herself as one of the crack ships in the trade. She is in first-class order throughout. Captain Davidson reports that he left the docks on October 7, and landed the pilot at the Start Point on the 10th, taking his departure on the following day. Variable winds were met with going across the Bay of Biscay, and a strong gale from the westward, lasting 48 hours, was encountered, but no damage was done, notwithstanding that a very high sea was running. The N.E. trades were fallen in with in 30° N., and 22° W., and proved moderate but steady to 9° N. and 26° W., when they gave out. From there had light and variable winds till the 9th November, when the Equator was crossed in longitude 30° W. The S.E. trades, which were got in 3° N., proved very good, and sent the ship along at a rattling pace to 29° S. and 28° W., thence variable and easterly winds were met with till passing the meridian of the Cape on December 2, in latitude 38½ S., when she commenced to make the easting. Fine fresh westerly winds were met with from the Cape up till the Otway was sighted on the 24th instant, the run having been made on the parallel of 43° S. The average speed from the Cape to the Otway was 266 miles daily. On the 10th December a gale sprang up from the northward, but afterwards veered round to the westward, and gradually increased in violence till the following day, when the foresail and the lower fore-topsail were carried away. Otherwise no damage was done, and comparatively little water was taken on deck.

Captain Davidson's Account of the Voyage
TROVE http://nla.gov.au/nla.news-article13523029

The Brilliant departed Sydney on 12th April 1883, with bales of wool and large quantities of other produce, for the return voyage to London. The passengers again included Captain Davidson's wife and child.

DEPARTURES.—April 12.

William Duthie, barque, 968 tons, Captain William M'Callum, for London. Passengers—Mr and Mrs C. W. Wilson.

Brilliant, ship, 1613 tons, Captain C. W. Davidson, for London. Passengers—Mrs Davidson and child, Miss Parkes, Mr C. S. Bowker.

Drumburton, ship, 1840 tons, Captain John Cowell, for

By 25th July 1883, the Brilliant had reached the Lizard near Falmouth, and continued on to dock in London, arriving back there on 7th August 1883, and cleared customs on the 8 August. After a lengthy voyage of 110 days port to port.

Brilliant Under Tow
Peninsular & Oriental Company (P&O) in the Background
State Library of Queensland

After the Brilliant docked, James was discharged in London on 7th August 1883, and paid the balance of his wages £8 - 18s.

Passage Report of the Brilliant from 1887

Passage reports were frequently published giving details of the voyages of clippers, some with little to report others with a graphic description of the storms they encountered. This lengthy report from the Brilliant's 1887 voyage, details what must have been a traumatic experience for the crew. (TROVE http://nla.gov.au/nla.news-article18965005)

A Rough Passage.

(From the Herald.)

The fine iron clipper Brilliant, one of the Duthie line, which has been expected in port any time during the past 20 days, arrived on Sunday from London, after a voyage of 99 days from Portland. The cause of the delay in the vessel's appearance was owing to her being dismasted in circumstances related below; and, considering the crippled state in which she has been since the accident, the performance is in every way creditable, and quite in keeping with her past record. Captain Charles Davidson, who is still in command, gives the following graphic narrative of the voyage:—"The Brilliant landed her pilot at Portland on August 24th, took her departure from the Lizard on August 26th. Gough Island was sighted on October 14th. October 19th began with a strong breeze blowing from S.S.W. with passing squalls and a high confused sea, the barometer rising steadily and gradually; at 3.30 a.m. the barometer stood at 30.28, and there was nothing in the appearance of the weather to indicate more than the ordinary squalls that had been passing all night, the ship going along with all sail, even to the main royal. At 3.40 a.m. a sudden heavy squall or violent gust of wind, struck the ship abeam with great force, and almost immediately the foretopmast carried away close to the lower cap, bringing down with it the foretopgallant and royal masts and yards and breaking the crane and standard of the lower topsail yard, and bringing it down also, leaving nothing aloft forward but the foreyard, the slings of which were badly strained. The maintopmast carried away close to the hounds, and slings of which were badly strained. The maintopmast carried away close to the hounds, and brought down with it the topgallant and royal masts and yards and upper main-topsail yard. On going forward to the forecastle, Captain Davidson found that the bobstay had parted, and that the bowsprit was sprung and broken, and only holding on apparently by part of one plate. The wreckage had all fallen overboard to leeward, on the port side, and in falling had struck and smashed the main rail and crushed the bulwark plates. Several of the chain-plates were broken off, and it had made a clean sweep of all the lanyards of the forerigging on that side. The main deck planking was stove in in several places, and the forecastle rail and covering board were broken. The wreckage was all towing to leeward, and every plunge was threatening to take away the jibboom and broken bowsprit. The ship lost her steerage way, and notwithstanding that all the mizen sails were taken in and stowed, she came to, and lay in the trough of the sea. Owing to the high, cross, confused sea, the wreckage was crashing and grinding alongside and under the ship's bottom, which it struck with tremendous blows, the ship plunging heavily on to it, and threatening to start the rivets or stave in the plates. Captain Davidson consulted with the officers, and decided (though with very great reluctance) that for the safety of the ship, the cargo, and all concerned, it was necessary to cut away part of the rigging, and let the wreckage go clear of the ship, which was accordingly done as promptly as possible, but not before the ship had received several very severe blows. They cut away all the foretopmast and topgallant and royal backstays, and all the headstays, main-topgallant and royal backstays, and all the running gear, with spars and sails attached. The wreckage then drifted clear of the ship, and she was got before the wind and sea. The carpenter sounded the pumps at short intervals, but found the vessel making no water. The Brilliant's position at the time of the accident was lat. 40·56 S., and long. 15·20 E., the Cape of Good Hope bearing N.N.E. 426 miles. The master decided to proceed on the voyage to Sydney, putting the ship under jury-rig to the best possible advantage with the spars, sails, &c., he had on board. The damage done, it is estimated, will take at least £3000 to make good; but had Captain Davidson put into Cape Town to have repairs effected, the expense to the insurers of the ship would most likely have been three times as much. After the accident the vessel laboured greatly, and it was almost marvellous that no one was hurt by the falling spars, especially as the watch was all on deck at the time. The Brilliant has travelled 7000 miles in her present state, and an evidence of saling qualities is to to be found that she traversed 270 miles in the 24 hours on two occasions after the accident. The easting was run down in 39° and 40° S. till in 80° E. longitude, and the remainder was run in 45°, with westerly

breezes. The South Cape of Tasmania was rounded on Saturday, November 26, with the wind strong from W.S.W., and heavy sea, the vessel shipping large quantities of water. This lasted up to Cape Howe, which was passed on the 29th ultimo, 100 miles to the eastward. The weather then became very unsettled, and the barometer unsteady, while there was a high cross sea, in which the Brilliant laboured very heavily. On Saturday morning the wind came away fresh from S.W., and carried the ship to the heads. She was towed in by the Irresistible, and anchored below Garden Island, having cartriges on board. Although the vessel is somewhat dilapidated-looking aloft, she presents the same bright and creditable appearance about the decks as ever.

Lloyd's Register Foundation, Report of Survey for Repairs for Brilliant 1882

ANNUAL SURVEYS.

41738

(Received at London Office) 15/9/82

No. Survey held at London Date, first Survey 12th September Last Survey 12th September 1882

(No. of Visits 1)

No. in Reg. Book 687 on the Iron Ship "Brilliant" Master C. W. Davidson

Tonnage: Net 1613, Gross 1666, Under Dk. 1488 — Built at Aberdeen When built (Year) 1877 (Month) 7th

By whom built J. Duthie, Ss & C. Owners J. Duthie, Sons & Co

Port belonging to Aberdeen. Destined Voyage Sydney.

If Surveyed Afloat or in Dry Dock In the Commercial Dry Dock. (State Name of Dock.)

Last Survey, No. 40538 Port of Lon — Classed (Years assigned / Character in Register Book) 100A.1 — S.S. Lon. No 1-81 — 6.81

Present Condition of the					
Decks	good	~~Treenails~~ Rivets	good		
Waterways	Do	Breasthooks and Stemson	Do	Windlass and Capstan	good
Comings	Do	Transoms, ~~Pointers~~, and Crutches	Do	Pumps	Do
Upper Deck Beams & Fastenings	Do	~~Timbers of~~ the Frame ~~at~~ the Openings	Do	Boats	Do
Lower Deck Beams & Fastenings	Do	~~Ditto~~ ditto at other places	Do	Masts, Yards, &c.	Do
Plankshears	Do	Keelsons	Do	Condition, how ascertained	from the deck
Sheerstrakes	Do	~~Clamps and Shelfs~~		Sails	good
Topsides	Do	Ceiling	Do	Anchors, No. of	3 B. 1 S. 2 K.
Wales	Do	Rudder	Do	Cables	Complete
Plating ~~Plank~~ (Bottom) and Counter	Do	~~Copper or Y.M.~~ ~~When put on~~		Hawsers and Warps	good
		Caulking of Bottom, Deck, & Waterways	good	Standing and Running Rigging	Do

~~Engine Room Skylights~~ ~~Coal Bunkers, Openings, Lids, &c.~~ Scuppers good Cargo and Main Hatchways good Hatches good

General Observations, Opinion as to Class, &c.
The bottom has been examined & coated. Vessel surveyed with ballast in the hold under the main hatch.
She is in good and efficient condition & eligible in my opinion to remain as classed.

Committee's Minute Tuesday, 19th September 18 82 — J. H. Truscott.

Surveyor to Lloyd's Register of British and Foreign Shipping.

Character assigned 100 A 1 TRW

Certificate (if required, to be sent as per margin) ____ Paid ____ 18__

No. Survey held at ____ Date, first Survey ____ Last Survey ____ 18__ (No. of Visits ____)

No. in Reg. Book. on the ____ Master ____

Tonnage (Net, Gross, Under Dk.) ____ Built at ____ When built (Year, Month) ____

By whom built ____ Owners ____

Port belonging to ____ Destined Voyage ____

If Surveyed Afloat or in Dry Dock ____ (State Name of Dock.)

Last Survey, No. ____ Port of ____ Classed (Years assigned / Character in Register Book) ____

Present Condition of the					
Decks		Treenails			
Waterways		Breasthooks and Stemson		Windlass and Capstan	
Comings		Transoms, Pointers, and Crutches		Pumps	
Upper Deck Beams & Fastenings		Timbers of the Frame at the Openings		Boats	
Lower Deck Beams & Fastenings		Ditto ditto at other places		Masts, Yards, &c.	
Plankshears		Keelsons		Condition, how ascertained	
Sheerstrakes		Clamps and Shelfs		Sails	
Topsides		Ceiling		Anchors, No. of	
Wales		Rudder		Cables	
Plank (Bottom) and Counter		Copper or Y.M. When put on		Hawsers and Warps	
		Caulking of Bottom, Deck, & Waterways		Standing and Running Rigging	

Engine Room Skylights ____ Coal Bunkers, Openings, Lids, &c. ____ Scuppers ____ Cargo and Main Hatchways ____ Hatches ____

General Observations, Opinion as to Class, &c.

Committee's Minute ____ 18__

Character assigned ____

Surveyor to Lloyd's Register of British and Foreign Shipping.

Certificate (if required, to be sent as per margin) ____ Paid ____ 18__

After a long and successful service on the Australia run, the Brilliant was eventually sold to the Italian company Tommaso Gazzolo, of Genoa in 1905, and was renamed Nostra Signora Del Carmine. Sadly, during the first world war, on 25th August 1916, she was sunk by the German submarine U-38, in the Gulf of Lyons, en-route from Baltimore to Genoa with a cargo of coal.

U-38 had the third highest U-boat kill rate during the first world war, sinking 139 merchant vessels and war ships. On this occasion the crew of the Nostra Signora Del Carmine, were allowed to leave the ship using their lifeboats which were later towed towards land by U-38. The doomed ship was sunk using thirty shells fired from the deck gun of U-38, saving their torpedoes for another attack.

The captain of the U-38, Max Valentiner, was born in Denmark in 1883, and had a formidable record of 144 ships sunk, 8 ships damaged, and 3 taken as prize.

The P&O passenger liner SS Persia didn't get the same courtesy when she was torpedoed without warning by U-38, on 30th December 1915. The ship sank in less than ten minutes, killing 343 of the 519 souls aboard, as only 4 lifeboats could be launched. At the time of sinking, SS Persia was carrying a large quantity of gold and jewels belonging to the Maharaja Jagatjit Singh.

U-38

The Ethiopian (Ship Number 48859)

The second ship appearing on the pension claim form, was the Aberdeen built Ethiopian. This was for another voyage to Sydney on the wool trade this time for the George Thompson Junior Company, Aberdeen White Star Line. His service was from May 1885 to January 1886, a relatively short trip.

'ETHIOPIAN'. 838 TONS

The Ethiopian was launched on 18th August 1864, from the Walter Hood & Co. shipyard in York Street, Footdee, in Aberdeen, she was christened by Miss Hopcraft. Designed for speed, the Ethiopian was originally built for the highly lucrative China tea run.

HEAVY STEAM WINDLASS

From the press report in the Aberdeen, Press and Journal on 24th August, the ship was fitted with what must have been leading technology of the day, including steam operated cranes, and windlass. Also importantly for the crew, water distilling apparatus.

The ship had 3 decks in total, a main deck, a half poop deck and a top gallant forecastle, There were 3 masts which were barque rigged, a round stern, carvel built, with a demi-female figurehead.

The Ethiopian had an interesting arrangement for her accommodation, which was placed in a large deckhouse extending from side to side. The rail was approximately 4ft 6ins above the deck and the sides of the house were rounded down on to the rail; just as in a poop deck extending right to the stern. But there was a gap between the rear end of the house and taff rail in which was a low deck occupied by the binnacle, wheel and wheel box.

The Ethiopian
National Maritime Museum (PAH0691)

To get forward from the wheel meant going up over the deck house by means of the ladders, or else down steps through the house and out on to the main deck. This arrangement was only found in a few sailing ships in the early 1860s. Although it can be seen in some steamers.

The Ethiopian was older and only half the tonnage of James' previous ship the Brilliant, it was originally built for the great tea run, along with the more publicised Cutty Sark and Thermopylae.

Several books on the clipper ship Shanghai to London tea races mention the Ethiopian, one interesting report from “The Log of the Cutty Sark” describes the rivalry between the ships captains.

Extract from: Basil Lubbock book “The Log of the Cutty Sark”

> *Shanghai Tea run races, Captain Dalrymple of the Duke of Abercorn was evidently full of confidence that his ship could beat any other ship in Shanghai on the race home to London. He proceeded to challenge every clipper which was going to load new teas. This sporting spirit led to a great deal of betting amongst the shipping fraternity, and finally the crews of the Cutty Sark, Duke of Abercorn, Serica, Forward Ho, Argonaut, Ethiopian and the John R. Worcester waged a month's pay, to go to the ship which made the quickest passage from Shanghai to the Channel. The race was won by the Cutty Sark.*

THE LOG OF
THE "CUTTY SARK"
By BASIL LUBBOCK

Voyage Details

James signed on in London on 5th May 1885 for the voyage on the Ethiopian, to Sydney.

Agreement and Account of Crew

Eng. 1.

Executed in Sixteen Pages.

C. R. S. & R. O. RECEIVED. 21 JAN. 86

Any Erasure, Interlineation, or Alteration in this Agreement will be void unless attested by some Superintendent of a Mercantile Marine Office, Officer of Customs, Consul, or Vice-Consul, to be made with the consent of the persons interested.

AGREEMENT AND ACCOUNT OF CREW.

FOREIGN-GOING SHIP.

The term "Foreign-going Ship" means every Ship employed in trading or going between some place or places in the United Kingdom and some place or places situate beyond the Coasts of the United Kingdom, the Islands of Guernsey, Jersey, Sark, Alderney, and Man, and the Continent of Europe between the River Elbe and Brest inclusive.

Name of Ship.	Official No.	Port of Registry.	Port No. and Date of Register.	Registered Tonnage Gross	Registered Tonnage Net	Nominal Horse power of Engines (if any).
Ethiopian	48859	Aberdeen	20 / 1864	838		✓

REGISTERED MANAGING OWNER.

Name.	Address. (State No. of House, Street, and Town.)	No. of Seamen for whom accommodation is certified. (30 & 31 Vict. c. 124.)	First Deck above it. ft.	in.	Second Deck above it. ft.	in.
Wm. Henderson	Aberdeen		4	3		

For the voyage on the Ethiopian, the ship's master was Captain Alexander Jenkyns, and the registered owner was William Henderson of Aberdeen. The voyage was to Sydney, but as was normal it could involve a wide range of oceans and continents, for up to two years and a return port anywhere in the UK. Being a relatively small vessel at 838 tons, the crew to safely sail the ship was only sixteen.

Sir William Henderson of Devanha.

Henderson was one of the partners in the Aberdeen White Star Line, and resided at Devanha House in Ferryhill, Aberdeen. He was a very successful business man, and was made Lord Provost of Aberdeen in 1886.

James signed the crew agreement in London, and received an advance of £2 on joining the ship. His monthly wage was £4 for the duration of the trip, with an allotment to his wife and family at home of £2 per month.

The crew agreement records that while in Sydney, three members of the crew were discharged with mutual consent, and that five deserted the ship. To bring the crew back to the required ships complement, nine new crew members were engaged at the port.

Their arrival in Sydney was recorded in the crew and passenger list, dated 13th August 1885. This was a voyage of 100 days. The captain's wife accompanied him on the trip.

The Crew List, completed on 13th August 1885, records the Ethiopian arriving in Sydney, with Alexander Jenkyns as Captain, and James as Sailmaker.

INWARD.

A LIST of the Crew and Passengers arrived in the Ship Ethiopean of A Jenkyns Master,
Burthen, Tons, from the Port of London to Sydney, New South Wales, 13 Aug 1885.

Seamen's Names.	Station.	Age.	Of what Nation.	Names of Passengers.	Description.	Remarks.
Charles Cameron	Mate	1861	Aberdeen	Mr W. B. Inglis	Gent	1-1 = 2
W. L. Burge	2nd Mate	1860	Clifton	Mrs A Jenkyns	—	
John Miller	Carp.	1863	Aberdeen			
Alex Middleton	Stewd	1862	"			
Joshua Scott	Cook	1831	Barbados			
James Macdonald	Bosn	1824	Aberdeen			
James Mackland	Sails	1858	"			
J. G. Perer	AB	1862	Hants			
Andrew Aitken	AB	1859	Aberdeen			
Andrew Anderson	AB	1860	Norway			
Robt McKay	AB	1861	Glasgow			
John Archer	AB	1842	Barbadoes			
Thomas Pennycait	AB	1859	Lpl			
John Harris	AB	1845	Ldon			
Frian Kerpe	AB	1861	Germany			
Wm Clarkan	AB	1854	Portsay			
A Baldwin	AB	1857	Jersey			
Frank Morice	AB	1850	Montreal			
George Woodcock	AB	1865	London			
Alfred Hottley	Aprentice	1866				
Walter Wightman		1867				
H R C Fletcher		1869				
G F S Allen		1869				

23

Alexander Jenkyns
Master

Transcript of Crew List

ETHIOPIAN

OF (UNSTATED), A. JENKYNS, MASTER, BURTHEN (UNSTATED) TONS
FROM THE PORT LONDON OF TO SYDNEY, NEW SOUTH WALES, 13TH AUG. 1885

Surname	Given name	Station	Age	Of what Nation	Status	Comments
JENKYNS	ALEXANDER	MASTER			CREW	
CAMERON	CHARLES	MATE	1861	ABERDEEN	CREW	
BURGE	W. J.	2ND MATE	1860	CLIFTON	CREW	
MILLER	JOHN	CARPENTER	1863	ABERDEEN	CREW	
MIDDLETON	ALEX	STEWARD	1862	ABERDEEN	CREW	
SCOTT	JOSHUA	COOK	1851	BARBADOS	CREW	
MACDONALD	JAMES	BOATSWAIN	1844	ABERDEEN	CREW	
MACKLAND	JAMES	SAILS	1858	ABERDEEN	CREW	
PERU	J. W.	A. B.	1862	HANTS	CREW	
AITKEN	ANDREW	A. B.	1859	ABERDEEN	CREW	
ANDERSON	ANDREW	A. B.	1860	NORWAY	CREW	
MCKAY	ROBERT	A. B.	1861	GLASGOW	CREW	
ARCHER	JOHN	A. B.	1841	BARBADOS	CREW	
PEMYCAIT	THOMAS	A. B.	1859	LIVERPOOL	CREW	
HARRIS	JOHN	A. B.	1845	LONDON	CREW	
WERPE	FRED	A. B.	1861	GERMANY	CREW	
GLARHAN	JOHN	A. B.	1854	PORTSAY	CREW	
BALDWIN	A.	A. B.	1857	JERSEY	CREW	
MORICE	FRANK	A. B.	1850	MONTREAL	CREW	
WOODCOCK	GEORGE	A. B.	1865	LONDON	CREW	
HOTTLEY	ALFRED	APPRENTICE	1866		CREW	
WIGHTMAN	WALTER	APPRENTICE	1867		CREW	
FLETCHER	H. R. E.	APPRENTICE	1869		CREW	
ALLEN	G. F. S.	APPRENTICE	1869		CREW	
INGLIS	W. G.	MR.			PASSENGER	
JENKYNS	A.	MRS.			PASSENGER	

The Ethiopian had an interesting cargo of building materials on this trip, these were clearly intended for an expanding city. The details were listed in the Sydney Morning Herald on 12th August 1885. http://nla.gov.au/nla.news-article28363693

IMPORTS.—August 11.

[A special charge is made for consignees' notices in this column.]

Ethiopian, from London ; 3046 bars and bundles iron, 762 rolls lead, 500 casks cement, 11 packages anchors, 50 casks putty, 250 packages paint, 50 lamp posts, 200 boxes tinplates, 250 packages pitch, 36 levers, 480 packages crossings, 42 bundles rails, 513 chairs, 25 pairs wheels and axles, 50,000 slates, 1 case steering wheels, 50 packages oilstores, 2 casks lifebuoys, 488 packages white lead, 13 packages machinery, 22 packages furniture, 21 packages printing material, 160 cases bottles, 35 packages rope, 300 cases brandy, 50 cases whisky, 80 tanks malt, 550 packages beer, 106 cases wine, 10 puncheons spirits, 4 packages cotton, 10 trunks boots and shoes, 1 tank cocoa, 125 packages drapery, 14 packages nitrate of soda, 42 cases glycerine, 575 packages oil, 1750 boxes candles, 100 cases sauces, 100 cases milk, 446 bottles in wicker, and a quantity of merchandise and sundries.

A reminder of the dangers facing the crew of clipper ships was reported in the Newcastle Morning Herald on 11th September 1885. The London crewman George Woodcock fell 18 feet into the hold of the Ethiopian suffering concussion of the brain. He was one of the crew members who eventually deserted the ship while in Sydney.

Accident.

George Woodcock fell down the hold of the ship Ethiopian 18 feet, and suffered concussion of the brain.

The return cargo for the Ethiopian consisted of, 3465 bales of wool, 311 casks of tallow, 1246 hides, 7 barrels of fleshings, and 11 barrels of glue pieces, as reported in The Daily Telegraph (Sydney) on 3rd October 1885.

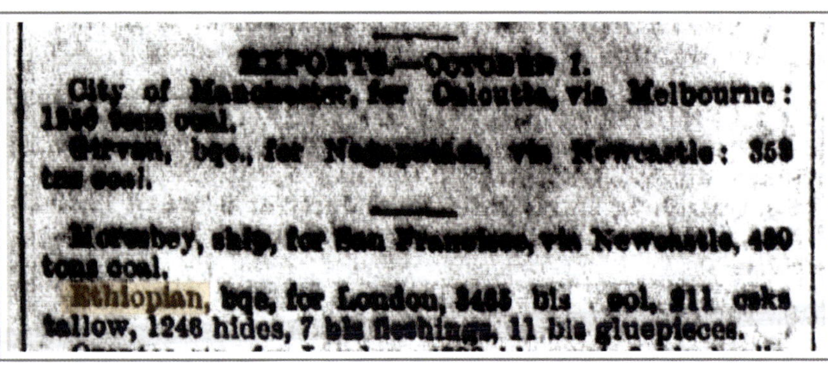

EXPORTS—OCTOBER 1.

City of Manchester, for Calcutta, via Melbourne: [illegible] tons coal.

Girvan, bqe., for [illegible], via Newcastle: 358 tons coal.

[illegible], ship, for San Francisco, via Newcastle, 400 tons coal.

Ethiopian, bqe, for London, 3465 bls wool, 311 csks tallow, 1246 hides, 7 bls fleshings, 11 bls gluepieces.

"SHIPPING." The Daily Telegraph (Sydney, NSW : 1883 - 1930) 3 October 1885: 4. Web. 29 Mar 2023 <http://nla.gov.au/nla.news-article237149016>.

following the loading of their cargo, the Ethiopian departed Sydney for London on 5th October 1885, this was reported in the Liverpool Shipping Telegraph and Daily Commercial Advertiser on Monday 30th November 1885.

After a lengthy voyage of 92 days the Ethiopian arrived back in London on 5th January 1886, discharging their crew on 6th January. James was paid £7 - 9s when he disembarked the ship in London, for his journey home to Aberdeen.

The London Wool Sales advertisement which appeared in the Maitland Mercury and Hunter River General Advertiser on 1st April 1886, offers cargoes from the Ethiopian and the Thermopylae to be tendered for sale in London, some apparently in rather poor condition.

Given the mixed cargo of hides and animal fleshings, it is not too surprising that some of the wool bales were contaminated, possibly due to storm damage.

London Wool Sales.

(From the Herald.)

Sale of 3673 bales, from Sydney and Queensland, by Charles Balme and Co., on Tuesday, January 26, 1886:—

Ex Ethiopian and Thermopylæ, from Sydney: AA&Co in diamond, 17 scoured fleece combings at 16½d, 21 at 15d; Payera, 23 scoured fleece combings hoggets at 15d, 12 fleece combing hoggets at 14d, 37 clothing fleece at 14d, 5 clothing hoggets at 13½d, 6 scoured damaged at 14d, 34 broken fleece at 13½d, 21 at 13d, 22 at 12½d, 1 damaged at 11d; Carwell, 2 grease part black at 10½d, 105 combings at 7d, 133 at 6½d, 129 at 6d, 15 combings hoggets at 6½d, 8 grease at 6d, 57 at 5½d, 38 damaged at 6d, 68 pieces part fleece at 5d, 2 damaged at 5d, 22 bellies at 4d, 2 locks at 2½d.

(http://nla.gov.au/nla.news-article18878498)

The flag of the White Star Line

After giving 30 years of service the Ethiopian was sold to Norwegian owners in Frederikstad.

When bound from St. Thomas to Cork, she was abandoned near the Azores (Western Islands). She was later picked up on 3rd October 1894 15 miles from Fayal and towed into St. Michael's, where she was condemned.

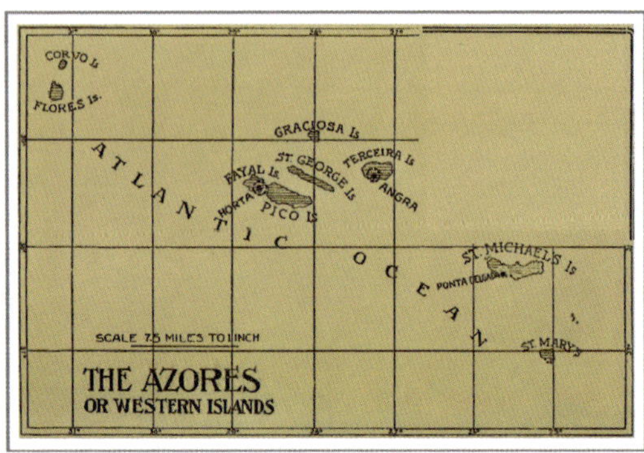

A Testimony to the Build Quality of Aberdeen Ships

Extract From Captain Falconer's log;

Thursday 7th March 1867 - Noon, heavy beam sea, ship rolling heavily and shipping much water on board. Latitude 16:50S, Longitude 170.10E, off New Hebrides.1pm increasing sea, ship not rolling so much, brought ship to close reefed main topsail, secured everything about deck and made snug for a fresh gale. At 4pm squalls increasing and a tremendous sea. At 4:30 blowing a severe gale, with rain and very heavy squalls, ship laying over with lee rails in the water. Main topsail blew out. Tried to get ship before the wind but she would not go off, being too far over. At 5pm blowing a furious hurricane, with incessant rain and heavy lightning, the sea a complete sheet of foam flying over the ship. At 5:30pm we were struck by an awful gust, which hove the ship right over on her beam ends, the sea half way over her deck, washing away everything off her deck. Ship appeared to be settling over slowly. All hands standing outside weather rails expecting they had only a few minutes left to live I ordered the mizzen & main mast to be cut away, which only required a few lanyards cut, when they went over the side. Still blowing furiously with tremendous sea. No sign of ship righting. Cut away the foremast, which appeared to ease her a little. Called the chief officer, Mr Anderson, but he could not be found. He was last seen going to cut away the main rigging, when he must have been washed over board. Other 3 were washed overboard, but succeeded in getting on board again. Carpenter reported that she had shifted her cargo and water was up to stringer on lee side. Sent all hands below to trim the coals. Gale decreasing but ship still laying over, with water getting into hold. Secured forecastle ports with sails. Hurricane overnight with wind, sea and rain which cut like a knife. Pitch dark except when lightning flashed. No-one on board expected to see morning. If ship had not been strong she would not have stood what she did. Cut away masts at 6:15. Daylight - got one of pumps to work & people trimming coals, but found ship helpless wreck. Only the bowsprit standing. Noon - ship righting and water decreasing. Hove overboard about 20 tons coals. Sunday 10th; very nearly upright, ship quite tight, under way with jury masts.

45915

REPORT of SURVEY for REPAIRS, &c.

Received in London Office, WEDNES. 3 MARCH 1886

No. in Reg. Book 786. Survey held at London. Date, First Survey 12th Feby. Last Survey 12th Feby. 1886. (No. of Visits) One

on the Wood Barque "ETHIOPIAN" Master Jenkins

TONNAGE: Net 839; Gross 839; Under Dk. 765

Built at Aberdeen. By whom Hood. When 1864, 8 (Year, Month). Owners G. Thompson & Co. Port belonging to Aberdeen.

Owners' Address (if not already recorded in Appendix to Register Book.)

If Surveyed Afloat or in Dry Dock: dry dock. Name of Dock: Thames Iron Works. Destined Voyage: Australia.

Length of Poop ft.: of Forecastle ft.: of Raised Qr. Deck ft.: Moulded Depth ft. ins. (If these particulars are not yet recorded in the Register Book.)

Classed: 12 A 1

Last Survey, No. 43738 Port Lon. Contd Aug 84–4. C 8 4.84

(State clearly the cause of Repairs if any, and, in detail, the nature and extent of Examinations and subsequent Repairs. Repairs on account of Damage should be separated from Repairs due to other causes. State also the dates and Initials of any letters respecting this case.)

Society's Freeboard (if assigned) as painted on Ship: in salt water ft. ins.; in fresh water ft. ins.

REPAIRS, OR EXAMINATION AS PER RULE: Condition

This Vessel has been examined in the Thames Iron Works graving dock. The metal found in good order has been patched in a few places and painted.

PRESENT CONDITION OF THE

Decks	good	Plank sides & Counter	good	Ceiling	good	Boats	4 good
Waterways	"	Treenails or Rivets		Rudder	"	Masts, Yards, &c.	"
Coamings	"	Breasthooks & Stemson	good	Windlass & Capstan	"	Condition, how ascertained	from deck
Upp'r Dk. Beams & Fastenings	"	Transoms, Pointers, & Crutches	"	Pumps	"	Sails	good
Low'r Dk. Beams & Fastenings	"	Timbers of Frame at the openings	"	Cement (if Iron Ship)		Anchors No. of	3B. 1S. 2K
Plankssheers	"	Ditto ditto at other places	"	Caulk'ng of Dk, & Watrwys	"	Cables	good
Sheerstrakes	"	Keelsons	"	Copper, or Y.M. (State if on Felt.)	"	Hawsers & Warps	
Topsides	"	Clamps & Shelfs	"	When put on	F & YM 4.84 see Register Book	Standing & Running Rigging	"
Wales	"						
Engine Room Skylights		Coal Bunker, Openings, Lids, &c.		Scuppers	good	Cargo & Main Hatchways	good
						Hatches	"

General Observations, Opinion as to Class, &c.:

This Vessel is now so far as seen in a sound and efficient condition, and eligible in my opinion to remain as classed.

Entry Fee (if chargeable) per Scale I., Sec. 27.	£	:	:
Office Fee (if chargeable) per Scale II., Sec. 27.	£	:	:
Survey Fee (per Section 28)	£	:	:
Special Damage Fee (if any) (per Sec. 28)	£	:	:
*Certificate (if required) to be sent as per margin	£	:	:
Travelling Expenses (if chargeable)	£	:	:
Second Surveyor's Fee (if any)	£	:	:

received by me, 188

Chas. B. Jordan
Surveyor to Lloyd's Register of British & Foreign Shipping.

Committee's Minute: FRIDAY 5 MARCH 1886

Character assigned: Contd 4 A 1

ROBERT EDMUND TAYLOR & SON, Commercial Steam Printers, 19, Old Street, Goswell Road, London.

The Ballochmyle (Ship Number 67930)

After completing his contracted service on the Ethiopian, James signed on as sailmaker for his next voyage on the Ballochmyle, a Dundee registered ship owned by David Bruce & Co., who operated the Dundee Clipper Line.

This would prove to be quite an adventurous voyage, calling in to the ports of Astoria and Portland on the West coast of America, after first delivering their cargo in Melbourne.

Ballochmyle about 1873

The ship was built for the original owners, McKeeler and Meldrum, in Sunderland by J. Watson & P. Mills. It was launched on 6th December 1873, and first registered in Greenock on 26th Jan 1874, its intended use was on the London to New Zealand route for emigrants. The ship changed hands several times before being taken over by David Bruce in 1884.

The Ballochmyle was a fast iron hulled, three mast clipper, originally build to carry large numbers of emigrants from the UK to New Zealand.

On her maiden voyage the Ballochmyle carried 502 passengers and 19 crew from London to Port Lyttelton, in Christchurch, New Zealand, under the command of Captain Loudon. The voyage commenced on 25th February 1874, arriving at Lyttelton, New Zealand on 1st June 1874.

Detailed listings of the 502 passengers appear in several family trees which have been compiled by the descendants of the original passengers. A short extract of one of these listing is attached showing the details of the family members, their ages, where they were from, their occupation, and the price paid for their voyage to a new life in New Zealand.

Extract From Ballochmyle Passenger List 1874

'Ballochmyle' when she left London on Feb 25th, 1874, under charter to the New Zealand Shipping Company, her destination being Lyttelton. She was a fine ship of 1,438 tons under the command of Captain LUNDEN. The immigrants came aboard at Plymouth and the ship took her final departure from Start Point on March 4th. The cape was rounded on March 18th and the Snares were passed on May 27th, the ship having taken 84 days from Plymouth. Port was reached on June 1st. There were 5 deaths and 3 births during the voyage.

The 'Ballochmyle' was the first vessel to berth at the breastwork, now known as Gladstone Pier. When she was taking her departure from Lyttelton, being towed out by the steamer 'Beautiful Star' the line parted and kicked back viciously. The end of the line struck Captain Hart of the 'Beautiful Star', breaking both legs. Capt. Hart was carried on to Dunedin where the steamer was bound but died before reaching port. The Southern paper, in noticing the death of Mr Thomas CARTER the old Pilot, in 1926, said it was Capt. LUNDEN of the 'Ballochmyle' who met with the accident but the victim was Capt. HART.

Extract from book 'White Wings, Vol.2, published 1928.

No.of adults	Name	Age	From	Occupation	Cost to Govt
2	GREEN, Thomas Elizabeth	37 36	Cornwall	Lab'r	£ 29
3	PREDDY, George Elizabeth Elizabeth Mark Jessie Alfred	32 36 5 ½ 4 2 ½ 7mos	Wilts	"	£ 50.15
2	PEARCE, John Frances John Frances	32 39 3 14	Cornwall	"	£ 43.10
2	COLENSO, James Elizabeth J	24 24	Cornwall	Navvy	£ 29
4 ½	BUTCHER, James Ann 38 Ellen 12 SW Benjamin 10 Emily 7 Julia 5 Florence 3 Charles 1	40	Hampshire	Lab'r	£ 79.13
3	MAJER, Charles Harriett 28 George 5 Albert 3	28	Northamptons.	Lab'r	£ 43.10

This interesting account of the Ballochmyle's first passenger voyage was published in the Christchurch news paper The Press on 3rd June 1874 when the ship arrived in New Zealand:

> *The ship signalled on Sunday proved to be the Ballochmyle from London with immigrants, she came up to an anchorage on Monday afternoon off Rhodes' Bay. The health officers, Dr Donald and Rouse, proceeded down to the vessel, and as there was no sickness on board she was at once cleared.*
>
> *The ship, which is new and on her maiden voyage, is a fine model, and is well fitted throughout, her cabins are roomy and well furnished, and she has a large poop cabin for the saloon passengers. The ship was built and launched in January last, and was built by William Watson, her length is 245 ft, beam 38 ft, between deck 9 ft, depth of hold 23 ft.*
>
> *On making the usual inspection, everything was found in admirable order. The emigrants Compartments throughout were scrupulously clean, the between deck lofty and well lighted and admirably ventilated. There was an improvement in the married persons compartment, the berths being high boarded and curtained, thus giving to married couple greater privacy. The ship has a large condenser, which has acted fairly during the passage, but a better galley for the emigrants should have been provided. The emigrants look extremely well, and appear excellently suited to the requirements of the colony.*
>
> *The surgeon superintendent Dr Smyth, is an old friend, he having come out with several emigrant ships, and in this case he has again been fortunate no disease having occurred during the voyage. During the passage five deaths occurred, three of infants from diarrhoea, and one from scald, a pannikin of boiling tea being accidentally knocked over on to it. One adult, a female, died from heart disease. There has been three births during the passage. The single girls who came out in charge of Mrs. Beardon are well spoken of.*
>
> *The voyage appears to have been a very pleasant one, concerts and amusements of various kinds having taken place during the afternoons. The ship was visited by the Commissioners and his Honor the Superintendent and Mr. Holloway. The latter expressed himself highly pleased with the arrangements, especially in the intermediate compartment.*

James added some additional details of this trip on the pension form; these were confirmed once a copy of the crew agreement was obtained.

This was for a voyage from Dundee to Fredrickstad in Norway, to load dressed timber, then on to Melbourne in Australia. From there the return voyage took them via Astoria and Portland in Oregon, USA, before their final UK destination of Liverpool.

This must have been a mammoth trip, and a long time away from home and his family, from signing on in Dundee to being discharged in Liverpool he spent 458 days on the Ballochmyle.

Ballochmyle

This voyage to Melbourne was a departure from the Ballochmyle's previous and next voyages which, as you would expect for a Dundee registered ship, were to Calcutta to load jute for the burgeoning mills in Dundee.

The Ballochmyle's home port of Dundee, was by the mid 1800s, dominated by the jute industry, relying on a steady stream of cargoes from Calcutta to keep the mills working.

Dundee Harbour 1888

The illustration of the Lochee, Camperdown Jute Works shows the impressive magnitude of the jute industry in Dundee.

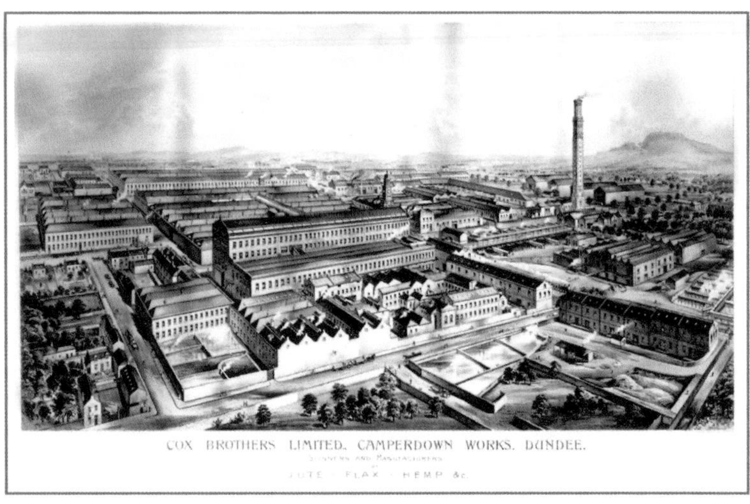

Camperdown Jute Works, Lochee, 1887
Reproduced courtesy of University of Dundee Archive Services

After a very spritely 100 day voyage from Calcutta, on it's previous voyage, the Ballochmyle returned to Dundee on 23rd March 1886, with a cargo of 9676 bales of jute. Following a quick turn-round the Ballochmyle was ready for James to depart Dundee on 12th April 1886 for another extended round the world voyage.

By all accounts it would appear that Captain Louden had some trouble enlisting a crew in Dundee for this trip. Several press reports document the unrest of the seamen, who were being offered £2-15s, per month for the trip. While at the Shipping Office they refused to sign the crew agreement for less than £3 per month.

Captain Louden was obviously not going to be held ransom by a bunch of rough sailors, so he proceeded to engage a new crew from the port of Glasgow, at the lower rate. When the new crew arrived to join the ship in Dundee several members of the Glasgow crew dropped out after being confronted by the original crew, who were looking for their solidarity in their claim for £3 per month.

SEAMEN'S WAGES IN DUNDEE.

The Dundee ship Ballochmyle has been detained in Dundee harbour for want of a full crew. Last week the master endeavoured to engage a crew in Dundee at £2 15s per month for a voyage to Frederickstadt, and thence to Melbourne, but the men refused these wages, and declined to sign articles under £3 a month. The master declared he would not give this sum, and sent to Glasgow to engage a crew at the reduced figure. He was successful in obtaining men there, and he brought them to Dundee on Saturday afternoon, but they had not been long in town when they were met by the Dundee seamen, who persuaded fully the half of them not to proceed. A number of men were subsequently engaged to fill the places of the absentees, and the ship proceeded on her voyage yesterday morning.

Shields Daily Gazette 13 April 1886

Checking the crew agreement it is apparent that three of the Glasgow crew failed to join the ship, and the others did indeed settle for £2-15s.

Agreement and Account of Crew

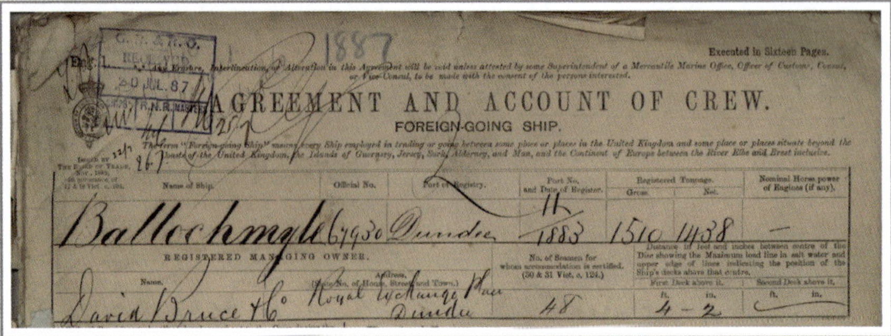

1887

Executed in Sixteen Pages.

AGREEMENT AND ACCOUNT OF CREW.

FOREIGN-GOING SHIP.

Name of Ship	Official No.	Port of Registry	Port No. and Date of Register	Registered Tonnage Gross	Registered Tonnage Net	Nominal Horse power of Engines (if any)
Ballochmyle	67930	Dundee	11 1883	1510	1438	—

REGISTERED MANAGING OWNER.

Name	Address	No. of Seamen for whom accommodation is certified. (30 & 31 Vict. c. 124.)	First Deck above it ft. in.	Second Deck above it ft. in.
David Bruce & Co	Royal Exchange Place Dundee	48	4 - 2	

For the voyage on the Ballochmyle, the ship's master was Captain Lundon, and the registered owner was David Bruce, with a registered address as the Royal Exchange Place, Dundee. The voyage to Melbourne, was to commence in Dundee, and after taking advantage of the wide description of ports of call they returned to Liverpool.

The Ballochmyle was another large vessel at 1510 tons requiring a crew of twenty four to manage the vessel. Unlike the other voyages, James has signed on this time for up to three years. The voyage was to commence on the river Tay, in Dundee, and initially on to Fredrickstad, in Norway, and thereafter to Melbourne, Australia.

The scope of the voyage then define that it can cover any port up to 75' North, and 65' South, which would cover most major ports in the world. The discharge port could be anywhere in the UK, or Continental Europe between the Elba and the Brest.

Several conditions were placed on the crew; if they were discharged at foreign ports, exchange rates were specified as two Shillings per Rupee for India, and five Shillings and six pence per Dollar for America. Any wage advances were to be charged a 5% commission. To discourage sailors leaving the ship before completing their contract, their wages were to be paid at a miserly one Shilling per month, if they were to be discharged at a foreign port.

James signed the crew agreement of 8th April 1886, and was contracted to join the ship at 6am on 10th April. James was paid £2-5s, for his first month, and £4-10s for subsequent months, with an allotment of £2-5s for his wife and family. On discharge in Liverpool after completion of the voyage he received the balance of his wages, £24-14s-5d, paid to an agent on his behalf.

The Voyage

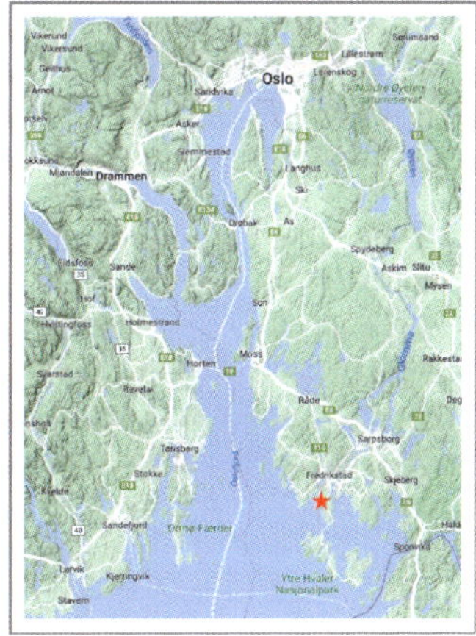

The Ballochmyles first port of call was at Fredrickstad, which is just south of Oslo on the Eastern entrance of the Oslo Fjord. This was to load their main cargo of dressed timber for the Australian burgeoning building industry. The crew agreement notes that one crew member left the ship and four new crew members joined the ship, as certified by the British Vice-Consulate in Fredrickstad, on 15th May.

They would have arrived in late April, press reports indicate after loading their cargo they departed for Melbourne on 29th May 1886.

The Ballochmyle took the great circle route around the Cape of Good Hope, and arrived in Melbourne after sailing for 116 days. The Melbourne Argos, reported the Ballochmyle arriving at Melbourne to offload their cargo of timber on 22nd September 1886.

SHIPPING TELEGRAMS.

(From Our Correspondents.)

PORT PHILLIP HEADS.

Arrived.—Sept. 22 — Ballochmyle, ship, from Frederickstadt.

Melbourne Harbour 1870s
State Library of South Australia (PRG1373/34/7)

During their time in Melbourne, there were several changes of crew recorded in the crew agreement. Five crew members were discharged with mutual consent, but without their wages, three others deserted the ship and were left behind in port. Seven new crew members signed the crew agreement, as witnessed by the Melbourne Government Shipping Master.

After discharging their cargo of timber at Melbourne, they loaded their new cargo for America, the Ballochmyle set sail for Astoria in Oregon, USA, on 6th November 1886 as reported in the Dundee Courier on 13th November that year.

The crew agreement records them arriving in Astoria on 3rd January 1887, presumably their first entry point to USA. The British Vice Consulate certified them arriving on 6th January 1887, at their main port of discharge, Portland.

LATEST ADVICES OF DUNDEE SAILING VESSELS.

BALLOCHMYLE, Loudon, at Portland (O.) from Melbourne, Jan. 5

Portland Harbour (1899)
Oregon History Project

Portland and Astoria are situated at the mouth of the Columbia River on the West coast of the USA.

Astoria and Portland

The ports of Astoria and Portland in the 1880s, were renowned for timber and canned salmon, both of which relied on the Columbia River. They were also at the end of the famous wagon road stretching 2170 miles from Missouri to Oregon's Willamette Valley, known as the Oregon Trail, which was in use well into the 1880s.

The ports of Astoria and Portland had a darker side, where hard pressed ships captains were desperate to replace crew members who had jumped ship after the long ocean crossings.

Shanghaiing was rife in both cities, the practice of kidnapping a man for service aboard a sailing ship. A shanghaied sailor, usually drunk or incapacitated by knockout drops, was delivered by a “Crimp”, for a fee, to a ship’s captain shortly before they were due to sail.

Astoria had a large immigrant, and transitional workforce of single men who filled the expansion of street-level watering holes, many of these housed what were politely deemed, “female-boarding-houses”. These saloons provided a ready source of unaware fodder for the unscrupulous Shanghaiers.

Also scattered around the waterfront were a number of sailors' boardinghouses. It was upon the proprietors of these hostels that the captains of windjammers sometimes relied to fill their crew, before departing on the next long ocean voyage.

During Astoria's zenith as a salmon canning and saw milling centre, a sound drink could be obtained at any number of establishments along the town's lengthy waterfront. But it was a stretch of Astor Street, that earned the distinction as “Swilltown”, a freewheeling strip that catered to all the needs and desires of loggers, fishers, and seafarers.

One such establishment was the Occidental Hotel built on wooden pilings over the tidal flats, dating from the early 1870s.

Astoria Occidental Hotel 1872
Oregon Historical Society Digital Archives

Portland also had their equivalent of Astoria’s Astor Street, in the form of a thriving China Town; which provided a similar service to transient workers and visiting seamen.

Chinese immigrants operated merchant businesses which were catering primarily to Chinese patrons, gambling and opium dens, and dwelling houses that served the short and longer-term housing needs.

The act of Shanghaiing, returned to Astoria once again in1984, when the Astor Street Opry Company premiered its melodrama "Shanghaied in Astoria" set in a bursting 1904 Astoria.

2022 Poster for Shanghaied in Autoria

Press reports show the Ballochmyle, leaving Astoria/Portland in early March1887, for Liverpool. Various reports quote 2nd, 4th, 5th March. The Dundee Courier on 9th April quotes the Ballochmyle leaving Portland on 4th March 1887.

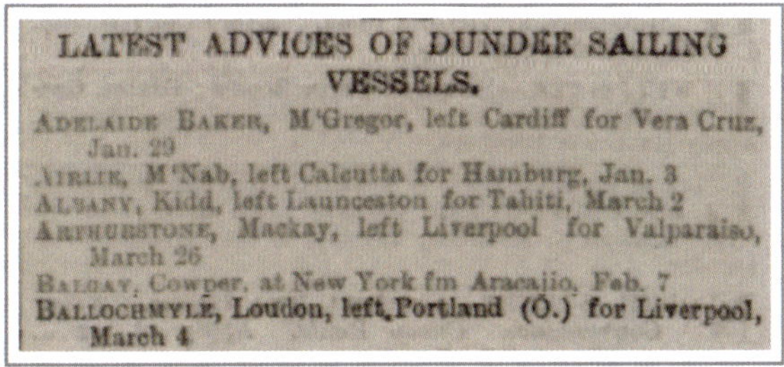

LATEST ADVICES OF DUNDEE SAILING VESSELS.

ADELAIDE BAKER, M'Gregor, left Cardiff for Vera Cruz, Jan. 29

AIRLIE, M'Nab, left Calcutta for Hamburg, Jan. 3

ALBANY, Kidd, left Launceston for Tahiti, March 2

ARTHURSTONE, Mackay, left Liverpool for Valparaiso, March 26

BALGAY, Cowper, at New York fm Aracajio, Feb. 7

BALLOCHMYLE, Loudon, left Portland (O.) for Liverpool, March 4

The Dundee Courier, gave a route report showing the Ballochmyle sighted at co-ordinates 47' North 19' West, on 5th July 1887.

They eventually arrived in Liverpool on 10th July 1887, after a return voyage round the infamous Cape Horn, in South America, a voyage of 123 days.

After giving reliable service for many years the Ballochmyle was taken out of UK service in 1897 when the British register closed, and was sold to foreign owners.

The vessel was sold in 1897, to B. Hansen of Stavanger, Norway, and renamed Hebe, and re-rigged as a barque. The vessel was sold again in 1901, to F. (Francesco) G. Leva, of Austria, and renamed Alba. It was then owned by the “Ship Alba Co. Ltd.” of Lussingrande, in Austro-Hungary (now Croatia). Alba was eventually converted to a hulk at Lussingrande in 1908.

Alba (formally Ballochmyle)

An earlier voyage of the Ballochmyle recorded some interesting events in the crew agreement. On this trip the deaths included one poor fellow, W. H. Peters, a 35 year old from Yarmouth, who fell overboard and drowned in the Calcutta, Hoogley River, on 15th December 1880. His belongings were sold, and the settlement for his account was £4-7s.

Calcutta Hoogley River 1890
British Library 15/1(85)

Another record on that trip certifies that six members of the crew were sent to the House of Correction, for six weeks, and left in Calcutta, for "refusal of duty". It does make you wonder about the moral of the crew under Captain Lunden. Their pay entitlement would have been converted to Rupees at two Shillings/Rupee.

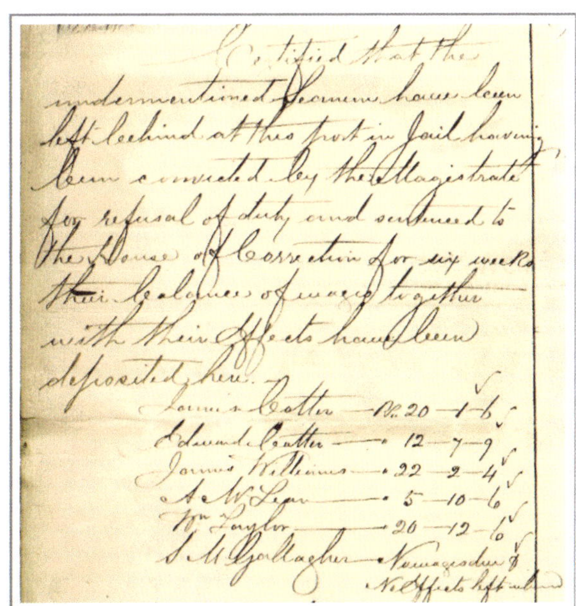

Certified that the undermentioned Seamen have been left behind at this port in Jail having been convicted by the Magistrate for refusal of duty and sentenced to the House of Correction for six weeks their balances of wages together with their Effects have been deposited here.

James Cotter — Rs. 20 — 1 — 6
Edward Coutter — 12 — 7 — 9
James Williams — 22 — 2 — 4
A. McLean — 5 — 10 — 6
Wm Taylor — 20 — 12 — 6
J. McGallagher — No wages due
No Effects left

49017

REPORT of SURVEY for REPAIRS, &c.

No. 41 Date of Writing Report 188 Port of London Received in London Office MON 24 DEC 1888

Survey held at London Date, First Survey Dec 1st Last Survey 18 Dec 1888

on the S. Ballochmyle Master

TONNAGE: NET 1438 GROSS 1511 UNDER DK. 1356

Built at Sunderland By whom W. Watson When 1873 12

Owners D. Bruce & Co Port belonging to Dundee

Owners' Address

If Surveyed Afloat or in Dry Dock Dry Dk Name of Dock Rugg's Destined Voyage

Length of Poop ft.: of Forecastle ft.: of Raised Qr. Deck ft.: Moulded Depth ft. ins.

Classed 100 A1

Last Survey, No. 3241 Port Liv S.S. Liv No 3 - 3.87 10.87

REPAIRS, OR EXAMINATION AS PER RULE, FOR Annual Survey

This vessel has now been placed in dry dock cleaned & restated. Rudder made good - portions of rigging & gear renewed & Equipment made good.

PRESENT CONDITION OF THE

	good	(Bottom) & Counter	good	Ceiling	ptl seen good	Boats	complete good
Ways	"	Rivets	ptl seen "	Rudder	"	Masts, Yards, &c.	"
ngs	"	Breasthooks & Stemson	not seen	Windlass & Capstan	"	Condition, how ascertained	fm deck
Dk. Beams & Fastenings	ptl seen "	Transoms, Pointers, & Crutches	"	Pumps	"	Sails	ptl seen good
Dk. Beams & Fastenings	" "	Frame at the openings	good	Cement (if Iron Ship)	not seen	Anchors No. of	3 13 15 24
Sheers	good			Caulking of Bot'm, Dk, & Watrwys	good	Cables	not seen - chain 15
Sheerstrakes	"	Keelsons	ptl seen "			Hawsers & Warps	complete good
Topsides	"	Clamps & Shelfs	" "			Standing & Running Rigging	good
Wales	"						

Engine Room Skylights — Coal Bunker, Openings, Lids, &c — Scuppers good Cargo & Main Hatchways good Hatches "

General Observations, Opinion as to Class, Recommendation, &c.:

This vessel appears to be in good condition & eligible, in my opinion, to remain as classed

Entry Fee (if chargeable) per Scale I., Sec. 27... £

Office Fee (if chargeable) per Scale II., Sec. 27... £

Survey Fee (per Section 28) ... £

Special on Damage, Fee (if any) ... £

*Certificate (if required) ... £

Travelling Expenses (if chargeable) ... £

Second Surveyor's Fee (if any) ... £

Fees applied for, 188

Received by me, 188

Geo. T. Cooper
Surveyor to Lloyd's Register of British & Foreign Shipping.

Committee's Minute THURS 27 DEC 1888

Character assigned 100A1

The Sophocles (Ship Number 77455)

James served on the Sophocles from July 1887, on a voyage to Sydney with Captain Alexander Smith. Given the transit time to and from Australia, we can assume that James was probably on a round trip on the Sophocles.

The Sophocles was an iron hulled clipper ship built by Walter Hood & Co, in Aberdeen, for George Thompson's Aberdeen White Star Line, it was launched in 2nd August 1879.

Length 223' 4" x breadth 34' 7" x depth 21' 7" gross tonnage 1176 tons.

The Sophocles was quoted as being a pretty little ship, though given a fuller body than Thompson's earlier ships as she was meant to be an economical carrier rather than a record breaker (114 days Sydney-London as member of Wool Fleet, 1888-9).

Sophocles at Sydney
National Library of Australia (PRG 1373/3/67)

This painting of the Sophocles berthed at Circular Quay in Sydney, was painted by its Captain Alexander Smith the ships master on James' voyage.

The Sophocles was part of the Aberdeen White Star Line and in this painting flies their house flag from the mainmast, and the red ensign from the mizzen. There is a grand looking steamship berthed opposite at West Circular Quay.

The painting which is signed in red on lower right corner, reads 'A Smith 1884' and is believed to have been painted for one of his passengers, the mother of Phyllis Lane, who was aboard the vessel on a voyage from London to Sydney that year.

Oil painting of The Sophocles at Circular Quay in Sydney
painted by Captain Alexander Smith on the 1884 voyage to Sydney

Sophocles Crew List Arrival at Sydney on 12th December 1887

No. 3842 Ret'd 13/12/87

A.—4.

INWARD.

A LIST of the Crew and Passengers arrived in the Ship "SOPHOCLES" of Aberdeen A. Smith Master, Burthen, 1120 Tons, from the Port of London to Sydney, New South Wales, 12th Decr 1887.

Seamen's Names.	Station.	Age.	Of what Nation.	Names of Passengers.	Description.	Remarks.
H. D. Clark	1st Mate	1848	British			
W. H. Rose	2nd Mate	1865	do			
Chas W. Wood	3rd Mate	1866	do			
Oskar Pettersen	Bosun	1858	Norwegian			
Wm Bartlett	Carpenter	1860	British			
Jas [illegible]	Sailmaker	1859	do			
Alexr [illegible]	Steward	1847	do			
Alfred Rock	Cook	1850	do			
Jack Holmes	A.B.	1853	Denmark			
John Sorensen	A.B.	1854	do			
Fedelrk Sorenson	A.B.	1837	do			
C. Johnson	A.B.	1855	do			
H. Daily	A.B.	1845	British			
W. Kenny	A.B.	1843	do			
H. W. Ford	A.B.	1866	do			
A. Schmidt	A.B.	1852	German			
Geo Rodegeore	A.B.	1806	British			
Geo Houlden	A.B.	1860	do			
A. Carlberg	A.B.	1857	German			
Geo. Heathcroft	A.B.	1867	British			
J. Sparkwood	A.B.	1855	do			
John Willcox	A.B.	1856	do			
C. Hughes	O.S.	1867	do			
J. Darcy	O.S.	1867	do			
Arthur Lewis	Boy	1870	do			
Jas Beattie	Boy	1871	do			
F. Hodgson	Cookmate	1871	do			
F. Robinson	Stowaway	1873	do			
Arthur Ball	Apprentice	1870	do			
[illegible] Crizelle	do	1872	do			
Wm John Brown	do	1870	do			
Guy Anderson	do	1867	do			

32

A Smith
Master

Transcript of Crew List

SOPHOCLES

OF ABERDEEN, A. SMITH, MASTER, BURTHEN 1120 TONS
FROM THE PORT OF LONDON TO SYDNEY, NEW SOUTH WALES, 12TH DECEMBER 1887

Surname	Given name	Station	Age	Of what Nation	Status	Comments
SMITH	A.	MASTER			CREW	
CLARK	H. D.	1ST MATE	1848	BRITISH	CREW	
ROSS	W. H.	2ND MATE	1865	BRITISH	CREW	
WOOD	CHAS W	3RD MATE	1868	BRITISH	CREW	
PETTERSEN	OSKAR	BOATSWAIN	1858	NORWAY	CREW	
BARTLETT	WM.	CARPENTER	1860	BRITISH	CREW	
MACKLAND	JAS.	SAILMAKER	1859	BRITISH	CREW	
NEVINS	ALEX	STEWARD	1847	BRITISH	CREW	
ROCK	ALFRED	COOK	1850	BRITISH	CREW	
HOLMES	JACK	A. B.	1853	DENMARK	CREW	
SWENSSEN	JOHN	A. B.	1854	DENMARK	CREW	
SWENSON	FREDRIK	A. B.	1837	DENMARK	CREW	
JOHNSON	C.	A. B.	1858	DENMARK	CREW	
DAILY	H.	A. B.	1845	BRITISH	CREW	
KENNY	W.	A. B.	1845	BRITISH	CREW	
FOX	H. W.	A. B.	1866	BRITISH	CREW	
SCHMIDT	H.	A. B.	1852	GERMAN	CREW	
REDMORE	GEO.	A. B.	1846	BRITISH	CREW	
HOULDEN	GEO.	A. B.	1860	BRITISH	CREW	
CARLBERG	A.	A. B.	1857	GERMAN	CREW	
HICKENOTT	GEO.	A. B.	1867	BRITISH	CREW	
FRESHWOLD	J.	A. B.	1855	BRITISH	CREW	
WILLSON	JOHN	A. B.	1856	BRITISH	CREW	
HUGHES	E	O. S.	1867	BRITISH	CREW	
DOREY	J.	O. S.	1867	BRITISH	CREW	
LEWIS	ARTHUR	BOY	1870	BRITISH	CREW	
BEATTIE	JAS.	BOY	1871	BRITISH	CREW	
HODGSON	P.	COOK'S MATE	1871	BRITISH	CREW	
ROBINSON	P.	STOWAWAY	1873	BRITISH	CREW	
BALL	ARTHUR	APPRENTICE	1870	BRITISH	CREW	
LINGELL	BENJM.	APPRENTICE	1872	BRITISH	CREW	
BROWN	WM. JOHN	APPRENTICE	1870	BRITISH	CREW	
SANDERSON	PERCY	APPRENTICE	1867	BRITISH	CREW	
WILD		MRS		ENGLISH	PASSENGER	
WILD	FANNY F			ENGLISH	PASSENGER	
WILD	THOS. H			ENGLISH	PASSENGER	
MCLAUGHLAN	T			IRISH	PASSENGER	
SHERRIFF		DR			PASSENGER	SURGEON
RYAN	D. L.				PASSENGER	JOURNALIST

Voyage Details

James signed the crew agreement in London on 23rd August 1887, for £4-10s per month, with an allotment for his family of £2-5s per month.

There were supposed to be six apprentices on the ship, however two failed to join the ship, and two replacements were found before the ship departed.

The Sophocles departed London at 4am on the 26th August 1887, after a lengthy voyage of 107 days, explained in the passage report, they eventually arrived in Sydney on 11th December 1887.

The passage report of James' voyage from London to Sydney was recorded under the heading of Maritime Miscellany, in the Sydney Evening News. (TROVE http://nla.gov.au/nla.news-article108222812)

THE SOPHOCLES.—The well-known trader Sophocles arrived from London, August 26, yesterday, and of the voyage Captain Alexander Smith reports that a quantity of adverse weather was met with, thus lengthening the voyage to 107 days. Owing to the heavy weather experienced in the English Channel, it was September 8 before she cleared it, and then light baffling winds occurred to Madeira. The equator was crossed on October 8, and the meridian of the Cape on November 5; Cape Leuwin was rounded on November 26, and South Cape on December 3. North-east gales were experienced on the coast. She brings a full general cargo, valued at £24,300. Her passengers are: Dr. Sherriff, Mr. Ryan, Mrs. Ould, Miss Ould, Master Ould, and Mr. M'Laghlan.

In Sydney one of the original apprentices deserted ship, along with two others, and eight crew members were discharged. Eight new crew members were engaged in Sydney for the homeward voyage.

After a quick turnaround, with a new cargo loaded, the Sophocles departed Sydney on 11th January 1888, for their return voyage to London. The Journalist Desmond Ryan who traveled out with them from London, was reported as the only passenger on the return voyage, his business in Sydney concluded on the short shore stay.

A brief report of their departure from Sydney was published in the Sydney Morning Herald. (TROVE http://nla.gov.au/nla.news-article13666669)

Sophocles, ship, 1120 tons, Captain Alexander Smith, for London. Passenger—Mr. Desmond Ryan.

James was discharged back in London on the 11th May 1888, with a final settlement of £14-9s-6d.

The passage report detailing James' return voyage to London shows the Sophocles experienced a succession of easterly gales passing New Zealand. They rounded Cape Horn on 27th February, and the equator on 23rd March. The voyage terminated in London on 21st April 1888, after what thankfully looked like a relatively uneventful voyage.

WEATHER AND NAVIGATION.

Dungeness, April 23.—The Sophocles, Smith, from Sydney (Jan. 11), arrived off here, reports:—After passing New Zealand experienced a succession of easterly gales, and Cape Horn was not rounded until the 27th Feb. Crossed the equator on the 23d March in long. 30 W. Had strong NE trades, and no calms after losing them. Had good westerly winds and made the Start on the 19th inst.

The Sophocles Return Passage Report

The Sophocles in the English Channel
Artist Roger Chapelet

Notable Sophocles Passage Reports

Over her life the Sophocles had many close encounters with storms, which claimed the lives of many crew members over the years.

This harrowing report of the Sophocles return voyage to London from Sydney in 1886, prior to James joining the ship, highlights the power of the sea and the fragility of the seamen.

The Sophocles Passage Report 1886

AN EVENTFUL PASSAGE.

The Sophocles (Smith) from Sydney, arrived in London, reports :—Left Sydney May 18, and had rather unfavourable winds rounding New Zealand On June 11 experienced a heavy gale from S.S.W., with a high sea; bar. 28 40. At 2 p.m., while running before it, shipped a sea on the starboard quarter, carrying away wheel, binnacle, compass, smashing skylight, &c.; J. Skinner, A B, was killed; Mr. Poppy, chief mate, was severely hurt; Mr. Sears, passenger, lost his left arm, and other two of the crew were slightly hurt. The same night, at 6 p.m., while lying hove to, the tiller carried away, and while trying to secure the rudder by means of chain strops round the rudder head and tackles on them, the master's fingers on the right hand were fractured, necessitating amputation. Passed Cape Horn on June 27, and crossed the Equator August 1, long. 26 30 W.

AN EVENTFUL VOYAGE.

The ship Sophocles, which arrived in Port Jackson on Monday *from London, which port she left* on June ,12 seems to have had a rough time during the passage. The officers on board, who have voyaged in the vessel for several years, state that they have no recollection of experiencing an unbroken spell of terrible gales for a period of seventeen days such as the ship has come through upon the present voyage. Upon one occasion the men lashed to the wheel of the vessel were torn from their position and washed completely over the wheel. Both were injured about the face and limbs, and *were rendered unfit for duty for some* time. The ship's ports, boats, and rail were smashed, and the doors at the entrance to the saloon repeatedly gave way before the fury of the sea that swept wildly along the decks, dashing into the cabins, which in some instances were knee-deep in water. The passengers and the crew, with the exceptions mentioned, escaped personal injury, however. This severe weather was experienced between the Cape of Good Hope and the Australian coast, and in the vessel's official report stress is laid upon the use of oil and its great value in reducing the height of the waves immediately around the ship. The testimony of the eye-witnesses is unanimous to the effect that the expenditure of the oil averted a great amount of damage to ship's fittngs.

A sailor named William Weller, died rather suddenly during the voyage from London to Sydney. He was shipped at Gravesend and formed one of a scratch crew made up for the vessel in consequence of a strike among the seamen at Home. Weller took his regular turn in the watches and appeared to go on well until June 18. On that date he complained of feeling unwell, suffering apparently from a cold in the chest. He was immediately knocked off duty, but took little or no rest till the following day, when he went off into a sound sleep and died. Captain Murray, the master of the vessel, examined the remains and found that the deceased was badly cut and bruised about the body, the injuries, which must have been inflicted before he joined the vessel, doubtless causing his death. Weller was a native of Clifton (England.)

After giving solid service for many years, as part of a divestment exercise initiated by increasing insurance premiums, the George Thompson Company sold the Sophocles to an Italian company in 1898.

In 1905 under the command of Captain Bersallo the ship suffered extensive storm damage.

A DISABLED BARQUE.

—:o:—

THE SOPHOCLES IN A SUDDEN GALE.

AN EXCITING EXPERIENCE.

MELBOURNE, Tuesday.

The barque Sophocles, which was bound from Adelaide to Falmouth with a cargo of wheat, was to-day towed into Hobson's Bay in a disabled condition. She had left Adelaide on the 26th March, but after experiencing four days' fine weather, a sudden squall of wind struck her. The gale was a fierce one, and came up from the south-south-west. All the canvas the vessel was carrying was carried away, while the foremast and the fore spars, and portion of the main mast were also unable to stand the sudden strain they were compelled to bear. They went overboard, and the mizzen mast was the only one left. The squall was as brief as it was fierce, and when it had passed over the appearance of the vessel had been entirely transformed. The wreckage was cleared away, and spare sails rigged upon the only remaining mast. One of the spars of the foremast had crashed through the men's deck-house, but nobody was injured through the impact. She made fair headway until she reached Cape Otway, where she was spoken to by the steamer Everton Grange. The captain asked that a tug be sent to his assistance, and when the steamer arrived at the Heads the tug Eagle was despatched. After picking up the vessel the Eagle towed her to port, and repairs will immediately be commenced. It is estimated that the expense will be considerable. The hull, however, was not injured during the storm. The Sophocles, which is a barque of 1351 tons, was at one time owned by the Aberdeen Company, but was sold by that company to an Italian company. She is now owned by Signor G. Balsa, of Genoa, and her master is Captain Bersallo.

Once again the construction quality of Aberdeen built ships stands out, as after repairs the renamed Sophocles went on to give several more years of solid service to the new owners.

The Sophocles After Storm In 1905, Anchored in Melbourne

The Italian owners, G. B. Olivari, registered the ship in Genoa, Italy and later converted the ship, for economy of crew, and management, and reconfigured the ship as a barque in 1910. The Sophocles was eventually broken up in 1925.

The Sophocles under Italian Ownership

The Soudan (Ship Number 91182)

The last voyage we have information on from the pension form, is the Liverpool registered ship the Soudan. This was a single trip from August 1891 through to October 1892, on the trade route to Calcutta, where it returned to the port of Hull with a cargo of wheat.

Calcutta Hooghly River 1890s

The ship master shown on crew list and the Lloyds registers, was Captain James Donald from Aberdeen, who was listed in the Post Office street directory of 1889-90, as residing at 36 Salisbury Terrace.

The iron ship Soudan was built for British & Eastern Shipping Co. Ltd., of Liverpool, and was completed in February 1885 at the shipyard of Richardson, Duck & Company Ltd., in Stockton, Teesside. The original port of registration on 24th February 1885, in the Lloyds Register of Shipping, was Liverpool, with Captain James Donald as the ships master.

Calcutta, now known at Kolkata

Agreement and Account of Crew

Executed in Sixteen Pages.

Eng. 1.

AGREEMENT AND ACCOUNT OF CREW.

FOREIGN-GOING SHIP.

FOR PARTICULARS AS TO LOAD LINE, SEE PAGE 15.

For the voyage on the Soudan, the ship's master was Captain James Donald from Aberdeen, and the registered owner was British and Eastern Shipping Company, with a registered address Liverpool. The voyage to Calcutta was to commence in Liverpool, and after taking advantage of the wide description of ports of call they returned to Hull.

The voyage was specifically from Liverpool to Calcutta, but could call at any port up to 72' North, and 65' South. The discharge port could be anywhere in the UK, or Continental Europe between the rivers Elba and the Brest.

The crew agreement specified that there would be no "Grog" onboard.

The crew agreement, highlighted the crew changes while in Calcutta, and tragically the death at sea of one of the three apprentices, nineteen year old Alfred Nicholson.

His obituary was published in the St. Austell Star on Friday 14th October 1892.

Intelligence has just reached Walreddon Manor of the untimely death of Alfred, fourth son of Rev. H. D. Nicholson. He was apprenticed in the Mercantile Marine to the British and Eastern Shipping Company, and was returning home from his fourth voyage to Calcutta in their fine ship Soudan. The captain reports that on September 24th, while blowing a gale with terrific squalls of wind, the unfortunate young man slipped and fell with one of the lee lurches, went through between the poop rails and instantly disappeared. This sad circumstance, an exact parallel to the case of General Elphinstone, not long since, will be a source of sincere regret to a large circle of friends of the family in the two counties. Mr. Nicholson was a former pupil at St. Austell School, where his amiable disposition made him a general favourite. His memory will be affectionately treasured by the "Old Boys" who were his contemporaries at school.

The outward bound crew list from Liverpool was found on the website of The National Archives, in Kew, Richmond.

Crew List of the Soudan - 1891

Soudan Crew List			
Ship: Soudan; Official number: 91182		**Age**	**place of birth**
James Donald	Master	42	Aberdeen
W Kelk	1st Mate	59	Liverpool
John McDonald	Carpenter	40	Durham
John Farrow	2nd mate	48	Dundee
Robert Gordon	Able Seaman	45	Aberdeen
John Campbell	Able Seaman	55	Dundee
Peter Fairley	Able Seaman	45	Dundee
John Bowen	Able Seaman	42	London
Emanel Carterge	Able Seaman	38	Smyrna
Daniel McKenzie	Able Seaman	36	Dundee
Thomas McKenzie	Able Seaman	45	Dundee
Thomson Ross	Able Seaman	28	Dundee
James King	Able Seaman	42	Montrose
James Wilkie	Cook	46	Dundee
Lewis Daguenorg	Steward	61	Calais
Alex Sidey	Able Seaman	32	Dundee
Alec Edwards	Boy	10	London
James Mackland	Sailmaker	59	Aberdeen
William A B Hammson	Apprentice	19	indentured 12 July 1887 in Liverpool
Alfred W Emmett	Apprentice	18	indentured 13 July 1887 in Liverpool
Alfred Nicholson	Apprentice	18	indentured 19 February 1889 in Liverpool

Note: The column Age has some as year of birth

James signed on in Liverpool for the voyage on 27th August 1891. His wages had now increased to £5 per month, with an advance of £2-10s, his wife and growing family had an allotment of £2-10s each month.

He was discharged in the port of Hull after fulfilling his contract, he was paid the final settlement of his wages which amounted to £32-4s-4d, it was paid to an agent on his behalf, and presumably made available to him in Aberdeen.

Voyage details to Calcutta

The previous voyage of the Soudan to Calcutta resulted in the ship sustaining substantial damage after grounding in the Hoougly river (detailed report attached).

This resulted in the ship spending some time in the graving dry docks in Birkenhead, before departing for Calcutta. Graving is an obsolete nautical term for the scraping, cleaning, painting, or tarring of the lower half of the hull of a ship.

Press reports show the ship being in the graving docks from late July 1891.

BIRKENHEAD GRAVING DOCKS.

CLOVER, CLAYTON, & CO.

Coniston Fell s 159 Bond, G Nelson & Sons ... —
Soudan 1699 Donald, British & Eastern Shipping Co .... —

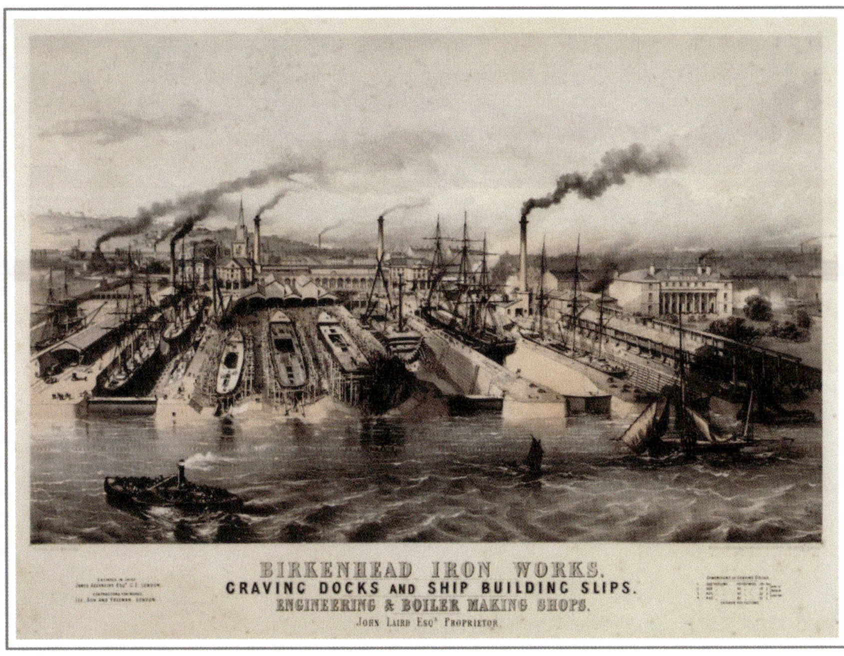
BIRKENHEAD IRON WORKS.
GRAVING DOCKS AND SHIP BUILDING SLIPS.
ENGINEERING & BOILER MAKING SHOPS.
JOHN LAIRD ESQ[R] PROPRIETOR.

Several press reports show that the Soudan was also in the Alfred graving dock, prior to their departure for Calcutta.

The Soudan, under the ownership of the British and Eastern Shipping Company, left Liverpool on 29th August 1891. No details of the cargo could be found.

After a long voyage of 143 days the Soudan's arrival in Calcutta was reported the day after in the Liverpool Shipping Telegraph and Daily Commercial Advertiser on Wednesday 20th January 1892. Telegraphic communications were obviously well established, to be able to report their arrival so quickly.

While located in Calcutta's Hooghly river it wasn't uncommon for ships to wait up to 10 weeks to get into the crowded docks at Calcutta to offload, and load their cargos. This was due to the large amount of shipping traffic moored in the river.

One account by a Royal Navy officer Donald Piercy on his voyage 1890-2, described the final approach to Calcutta, from Garden Reach:

> *"proceeded past the magnificent palace of the King of Oudh, now going to wrack and ruin. Shortly afterwards on turning a bend, we came in sight of a forest of masts - Calcutta"*

At this time Calcutta was suffering a large number of deaths from Cholera, up to 300 a day. This macabre report from the Indian Medical Gazette highlighted cholera as one of the main causes of mortality among British seamen in the mid-nineteenth century:

> *"Seamen's health in the tropics had been a contentious issue for the British Empire. So it was probably safer to stay on the ship rather and venture ashore"*

The crew agreement documents five of the crew being discharged in the port of Calcutta, on 4th April 1892. This included the Scandinavian contingent consisting of two Swedes, a Dane, and one Finnish crewman. Presumably they were looking to transfer to another ship with a onward destination better suited to their home location.

The crew were supplemented for the homeward voyage to Hull, with five new members who joined the ship on 16th May 1892, as certified by the Shipping Master of the Government Shipping Office Calcutta.

The Soudan's departure from Calcutta on 22nd May 1892, was reported in Liverpool Shipping Telegraph and Daily Commercial Advertiser on Tuesday 24th May 1892.

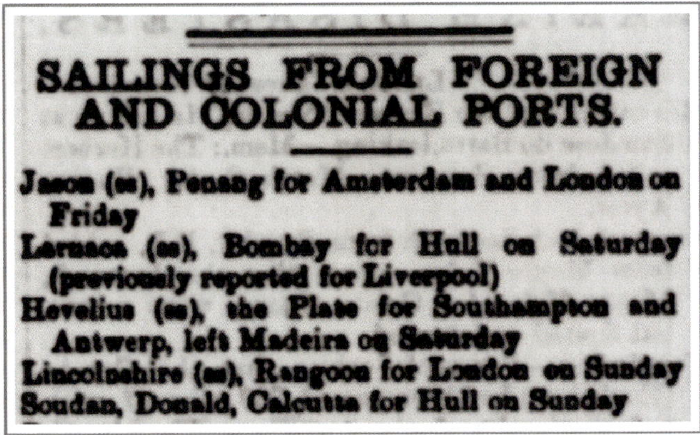

SAILINGS FROM FOREIGN AND COLONIAL PORTS.

Jason (ss), Penang for Amsterdam and London on Friday

Larnaca (ss), Bombay for Hull on Saturday (previously reported for Liverpool)

Hevelius (ss), the Plate for Southampton and Antwerp, left Madeira on Saturday

Lincolnshire (ss), Rangoon for London on Sunday

Soudan, Donald, Calcutta for Hull on Sunday

On route back to the UK, the Soudan stopped off at St Helena, in the South Atlantic, to replenish provisions, and left there in late August.

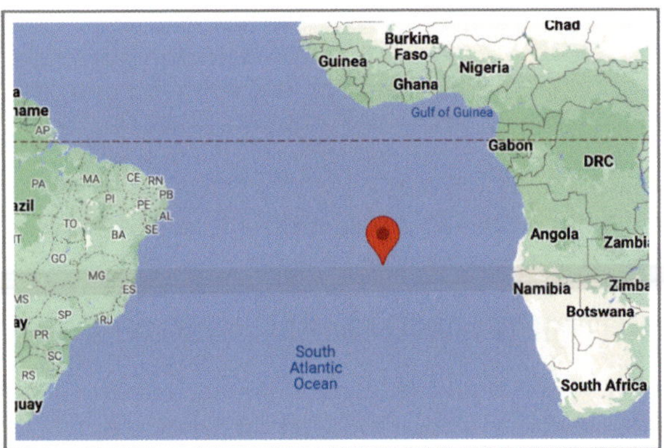

Having departed Calcutta, the Soudan arrived in the port of Hull with a cargo of Wheat, on 5th October 1892, after a voyage of 136 days. The arrival was reported in the Lloyd's List on Thursday 6th October 1892.

LATEST SHIPPING INTELLIGENCE.

ARRIVALS.

OCT. 5.—Soudan, from Calcutta, at Hull; Carlton, from Calcutta, at Lynn.

Home News for India, China and the Colonies

Friday 07 October 1892

Account of The Soudan's previous voyage to Calcutta.

This interesting account of the previous voyage to Calcutta, really highlights the hazardous sandbanks on the Hooghly river.

After a lengthy stay in Calcutta, the Soudan set off on their return journey to Dundee on Thursday 30th October 1890, but the ship was soon beset with problems which significantly delayed their departure.

During the week of the Soudan's departure from Calcutta the Hooghly river suffered from shifting sandbanks and mud flats, which resulted in a number of ships running aground over a period of several days. Being one of the larger ships at 1699 tons unladen, and capable of carrying a cargo of 2500 tons, the Soudan grounded on the tail of College Sands at Garden Reach. At the time of the grounding the ship was under the supervision of an assistant Harbour Master, while navigating the fast flowing Hooghly river to reach the open sea.

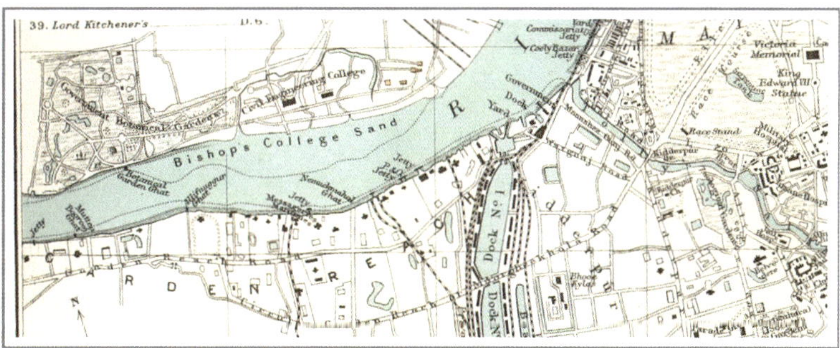

Garden Reach on the Hooghly River
(British Painter William Prinsep)

On the Thursday night the Soudan was towed off the sandbank with the assistance of an anchor boat, and tug steamer, luckily, without sustaining any damage. By all accounts the sandbanks on the Hooghly river were renowned for shifting, even in the space of a few days, which would easily catch out the best of river Pilots.

However, when the Soudan resumed their departure on Friday 31st October, one of the other grounded ships, the Polymina, ran into problems while under tow by the tug Retriever, and ran aground when their hawser parted.

Unfortunately this caused the Soudan to run aground for a second time on a bank above Anchoring Creek, where she remained stranded until the Sunday evening, when the tug Rescue, managed to get her off the sandbank. On the Monday she was towed to Diamond Harbour to survey the damage, where the crew began unloading her cargo of jute into lighters (barges).

Calcutta Harbour with Lighters (barges)

The Lloyds List of Wrecks and Casualties states that the Soudan was badly strained after the second grounding and had to turn back to Calcutta for repairs.

This accounts for the later departure of the Soudan, on 30th November 1890, a month behind schedule, was reported in the Englishman's Overland Mail on Wednesday 3rd December 1890.

ACCIDENTS IN THE HUGHLI.

There have been an unusual number of groundings in the Hughli during the past week, which probably in some of the cases were attributable to the shifting of the treacherous sands and mud flats of the river. All the vessels were large cargo ones. First there was the ship County of Haddington, in tow of the Alexandra, which grounded in Palm Tree Track, Nynan, on Thursday, the 30th of October, the track having silted up since the last report. She remained ashore until the high water of Friday, when she was owed off. Next came the ship Soudan, which grounded on the tail of College Sand in Garden Reach on Thursday night, and was towed off with the assistance of an anchor boat and tug steamer on Friday. The third was the ship Polymnia, in tow of the Retriever, which took the ground on on the left bank above Roychuck Tree. She was towed off at high water and went to Diamond Harbour on Friday, th 31st; but on proceeding up next day ill luck again attended her, and she took the ground while crossing out in the Nynan track. She did not stop, although she parted hawsers before she got straightened up in deep water. Grounding, however, as she did, in a narrow track, caused the ship Soudan to ground also, and this latter vessel took the bank above Anchoring Creek, and remained ashore until Sunday evening, when her tug, the Rescue, managed to get her off. On Monday she was towed to Diamond Harbour, where she is now discharging her cargo into lighters. She is probably strained by her severe experience, and may have to be docked and examined before being allowed to proceed on her voyage.

The ship Godiva is still in moorings at Garden Reach, repairing her damaged rudder, and it will probably be some days before she can be got ready. It will be remembered that some days ago she drifted over a mooring buoy when in the act of turning to proceed to sea from the Reach. The Tidal Report shows that the obstruction at Nynan is fast clearing away.

MAP OF CALCUTTA AND HOOGHLY RIVER

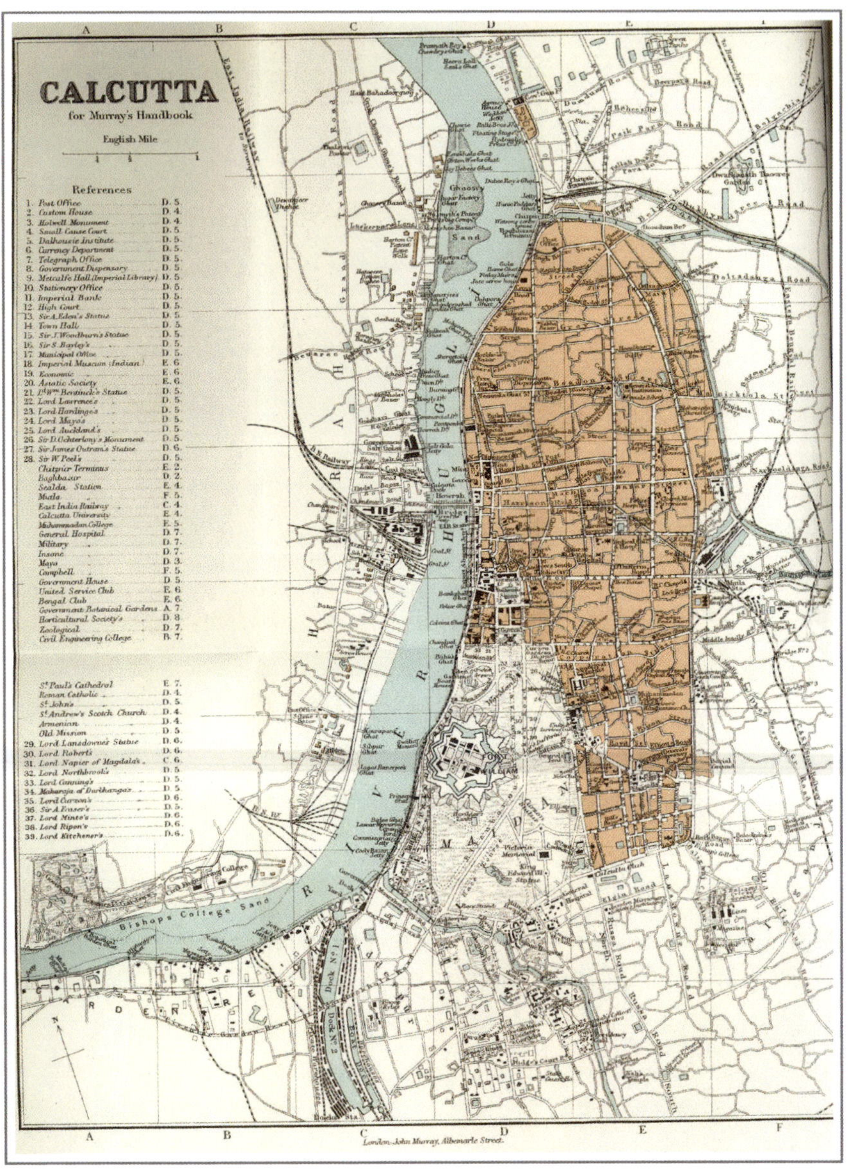

Lloyd's Register Foundation, Report of Survey for Repairs for Sophocles - 1888

REPORT of SURVEY for REPAIRS, &c.

No. ... Date of Writing Report 29 May 1888 Port of London — Received in London Office, WED 30 MAY 88

No. in Reg. Book. Survey held at London Date, First Survey 25 May Last Survey 29 May 1888

797 on the Iron S. Sophocles Master Smith

TONNAGE:— NET 1120 GROSS 1176 UNDER DK. 1612

Built at Aberdeen By whom Hood When 1879

Owners G. Thompson & Co Port belonging to Aberdeen

Owners' Address (if not already recorded in Appendix to Register Book.)

If Surveyed Afloat or in Dry Dock Dry Name of Dock Canal Destined Voyage Sydney

Length of Poop ft.: of Forecastle ft.: of Raised Qr. Deck ft.: Moulded Depth ft. ins. (if these particulars are not yet recorded in the Register Book.)

Classed 100 A1 8, 87

Last Survey, No. 47498 Port Lon S.S. Lon 102-87

State clearly the cause of Repairs if any, and, in detail, the nature and extent of Examinations and subsequent Repairs. Repairs on account of Damage should be separated from Repairs due to other causes. State also the dates and Initials of any letters respecting this case.

Society's Freeboard (if assigned) as painted on Ship: in Summer ft. ins. in Winter ft. ins.

REPAIRS, OR EXAMINATION AS PER RULE, FOR Condition

Vessel placed in dry dock cleaned down and recoated, & rudder rebushed bottom outside in good condition. Several loose rivets in rudder renewed.

PRESENT CONDITION OF THE

Decks	good	Plates (Bottom) & Counter	good	Ceiling	good	Boats	Complete & good
Waterways	"	Treenails or Rivets	"	Rudder	"	Masts, Yards, &c.	"
Openings	"	Breasthooks & Stemson	"	Windlass & Capstan	"	Condition, how ascertained	from deck
Upr Dk. Beams & Fasten'ngs	"	Transoms, Pointers, & Crutches	"	Pumps	"	Sails	Complete & good
Low'r Dk. Beams & Fastenings	"	Timbers of Frame at the openings	"	Cement (if Iron Ship)	"	Anchors No. of	3B 1S 2K
Plankshears	"	Ditto ditto at other places	"	Caulk'ng of Bot'm, D'k, & Watrwys	"	Cables	Not ranged
Sheerstrakes	"	Keelsons	"	Copper or Y.M. (State if on Felt.) When put on		Hawsers & Warps	Complete good
Topsides	"	Clamps & Shelfs	"			Standing & Running Rigging	"
Spales	"						

Engine Room Skylights — Coal Bunker, Openings, Lids, &c. Scuppers good Cargo & Main Hatchways good Hatches "

General Observations, Opinion as to Class, Recommendation, &c.:

This vessel now appears in a sound & efficient condition eligible in my opinion to remain as classed

Entry Fee (if chargeable) per Scale I., Sec. 27...	£	:	:	Fees applied for, 188
Do. Fee (if chargeable) per Scale II., Sec. 27...	£	:	:	
Survey Fee (per Section 28)	£	:	:	Received by me, 188
Special on Damage, Fee (if any) (per Sec. 28)	£	:	:	
*Certificate (if required) to be sent as per margin	£	:	:	
Travelling Expenses (if chargeable)	£	:	:	
Second Surveyor's Fee (if any)	£	:	:	

Thos. L. Gray
Surveyor to Lloyd's Register of British & Foreign Shipping.

Committee's Minute FRIDAY 1 JUNE 1888

Character assigned 100 A1

Wreck of the Soudan 1896

Five years after James left the ship, the Soudan while under full sail on route from Leith to Rio de Janeiro, carrying a cargo of 2540 tons of coal, was wrecked on 7th November 1896 after stranding on the outer side of the Scroby Sands, off Yarmouth.

A summary of the grounding and subsequent storm which caused the ship to breakup, was published in the Globe on Saturday 30th January 1897.

During the gale which lasted from the 7th to the 9th of November, 17 lifeboats were launched for wreck service, 12 of which were stationed between Happisburgh, in Norfolk, and Margate. Most excellent work was done by the Caister No. 2 and Gorleston No. 1 lifeboats to the full-rigged ship Soudan, which had stranded on the outer side of the Scroby Sand, off Yarmouth. An attempt was at first made to save the vessel, but when that easterly gale sprang up it soon became evident that the unfortunate vessel was doomed, and the Gorleston boat with difficulty rescued 19 of the vessel's crew and eight lifeboat men who had been at work on board the vessel. The lifeboat then lost her communication with the Soudan, leaving eight men still on board her, who were rescued in very brilliant style by the Caister No. 2 lifeboat.

A fuller account of the heroic rescue of the crew was printed in the Lifeboat Journal of 1897, giving graphic detail of the bravery of the lifeboat crews.

The Soudan was still under the ownership of the British & Eastern Shipping Company Ltd., when it's fate was sealed on 7th November 1896. The salvage value of the Soudan was set at a pitiful £7.

A Board of Trade inquiry was set up to ascertain the circumstances leading up to the grounding, which happened during calm weather, before the storm.

The ship's master, and the pilot who was onboard at the time of the grounding, blamed a faulty compass for the incident. However the court found the pilot George Combe negligent; the ships master Thomas Thomas could not be free of blame as he had the ultimate responsibility for the vessel.

East Anglian Daily Times on Friday 18th December 1896 reported that the master was suspended from duty for three months, and the pilot fined £20 for his failings.

It is interesting to note that before the storm hit, the ship's master had managed to go onshore in one of the lifeboats to consult with Lloyds Insurers as to what should be done to save the ship.

THE STRANDING OF THE SOUDAN

BOARD OF TRADE INQUIRY.

Mr. W. J. Stewart, stipendiary magistrate, assisted by Captains Anderson and E. Brooks, nautical assessors, opened a Board of Trade inquiry in the Magistrates'-room, Dale-street, Liverpool, yesterday, into the circumstances attending the stranding and loss of the British sailing ship Soudan, of Liverpool, on November 7, near the Scroby Sands, off Great Yarmouth. Mr. Paxton appeared for the Board of Trade, Mr. Weightman for the master and owners, and Mr. Edgecombe for the second mate.

Mr. Paxton stated that the Soudan was a vessel with a registered tonnage of 1,659, and was owned by the British Eastern Shipping Company, Limited, Mr. James Macdonald, Cook-street, Liverpool, being the registered manager. The vessel left Leith for Rio on November 4 last with a crew of 27 hands and a pilot. She had a cargo of 2,540 tons of coal. Early on the morning of November 7 a fog-horn was heard which was supposed to be from the Newark light, and shortly afterwards the vessel went ashore on the Scroby Sands, near Yarmouth. The master, Thomas Thomas, attempted to back her off, but failing in this he made signals for assistance, in response to which a lifeboat went out from Newark. Three tugs were sent from Yarmouth, and they attempted to tow the Soudan off, but failed to move the ship. The weather up to this time had been fine, but a gale suddenly sprang up, and the coxswain of the lifeboat advised the crew to leave the ship. The officers resolved to remain by the ship, but the others went off in the lifeboat. Later on the masts and rigging were carried away, and the officers were eventually taken off by the Caistor lifeboat, so that no lives were lost. The vessel, however, became a total loss. The pilot attributed the disaster to the compass not being correct, but the master did not agree with that view. No allowance had been made for the ebb tide, which would, no doubt, tend to put the vessel on the coast of Norfolk. She must have got to where she stranded either through an error in compasses, or to the ebb tide taking them over, or to bad steering.

Thomas Thomas, the master of the Soudan, narrated the circumstances of the casualty, and stated that the wreck was sold and realized only £7. He attributed the stranding of the vessel to her having been carried inshore by the influence of the tide.

Charles Combe, the pilot, who was on board at the time of the stranding, also gave evidence. He said he could offer no theory as to the cause of the stranding, but, questioned by the Court, he admitted that in the calculation he had made he had expected to pass four or five miles to the eastward of the Cross Sands Lightship, whereas in fact the vessel stranded about a mile and a half to the westward of the lightship. Asked if he suggested that the tide alone had carried the vessel some seven miles out of her expected course, the witness did not give any answer.

The inquiry will be resumed to-day.

Account of the Rescue of the Soudan Crew

Nov. 7.—CAISTER, NORFOLK, and GORLESTON, SUFFOLK.—*Beauchamp* and *Mark Lane* Life-boats.—In the afternoon,

during hazy weather, signal guns were heard from the St. Nicholas Lightship off the coast of Norfolk, in response to which the Gorleston Life-boat was launched and proceeded to the Lightship, when it was ascertained that guns had been heard to the eastward. At once the Life-boat was taken in that direction, and proceeding over the Scroby Sands she found on the outside of the Sand a full-rigged ship, named the *Soudan*, of Liverpool, 1659 tons, bound from Leith to Rio de Janeiro with a cargo of coal, and having a crew of twenty-seven men and a pilot on board. By request of the master the Life-boat returned for the assistance of steam-tugs, and every effort without effect was made to save the ship. The weather then got much worse, the wind ultimately increasing to a whole gale, accompanied by a very heavy sea, and at 6.45 on the morning of the 8th November nineteen of the ship's crew were taken into the Life-boat along with eight of her own crew who had gone on board to help in throwing cargo overboard so as to lighten the vessel; the captain had previously gone ashore to consult with Lloyd's agent as to the steps to be taken to try to save the ship. The Life-boat then remained at anchor close by for a time, after which she again bore down on the wreck and endeavoured to take off the remaining eight men, but could not manage it, as every rope broke, owing to the severity of the gale. Fortunately the Caister No. 2 Life-boat, the *Beauchamp*, had been launched in reply to signals a few hours previously after very hard work, some of the heaviest seas ever remembered being shipped, which thoroughly drenched the men, who experienced similar treatment in crossing the Barber Sands. They found that the only way to fetch the wreck was through half-a-mile of heavy broken water on the Scroby Sands, through which they proceeded, all hands lashing themselves in the boat. They arrived there about 7 o'clock, and the *Mark Lane* Life-boat, which was there waiting at anchor a little way from the wreck, sailed for harbour, her coxswain and crew having by that time been afloat in the boat for about nineteen hours.

With the help of a steam-tug and the use of her own sails the Caister Life-boat after some time was enabled to approach the wreck, but could not get alongside, the heavy seas knocking her away time after time, until lines had been passed to her by the aid of Life-buoys thrown from the ship. The crew were then enabled to haul her up to the stern, when she was swept under the lee quarter amongst the wreckage and the eight men jumped into her amidships. Having accomplished her mission the Life-boat made for harbour under sail and safely landed the rescued men at Gorleston. The latter part of this service taking place in daylight, thousands of persons watched it from the beach at Great Yarmouth, and as the boat made the harbour both piers were thronged with spectators, who cheered lustily. Thanks to the determined and brave efforts of the Life-boat men, the loss of this vessel was happily unattended by any loss of life. A relative of one of those saved by the *Mark Lane* Life-boat voluntarily forwarded the crew of that boat 5*l.* "*as a small recognition of gallant services, with heartfelt thanks.*"—Expenses of service, 109*l.* 13*s.*

Bauchamp Lifeboat Wreck 1901

Tragically one of the lifeboats that went to the rescued the crew of the Soudan in 1896, was overturned almost exactly five years later while on another rescue, sadly with the loss of nine of the crew.

Wreck of the Bauchamp Lifeboat

On the 13th November 1901 the crew of the Caister lifeboat Beauchamp was alerted to a vessel grounded on the Barber Sands. Gale force winds made the launch near impossible taking three hours to get the boat away.

One hour later the Beauchamp was found overturned near the shoreline and the crew trapped underneath. Seventy-eight year old James Haylett Senior, a former assistant coxswain, and his grandson Frederick Haylett raced to the scene. They managed to save three of the twelve man crew.

Haylett Senior received the RNLI Gold Medal for Gallantry. When asked if he thought the crew had abandoned the rescue attempt before capsizing he is said to have replied “Caister Men never turn back”. These words became the motto for Caister lifeboat station.

The Last Commercial Windjammers

Surprisingly, the commercial working life of the great iron hulled windjammers only came to an end in 1949.

By the 1890s improvements in the design of steam engines and the opening of the Suez Canal, made the steamship a more efficient cargo carrier than sail. If it hadn't been for Gustav Erickson, an Aland Islander, who was able to build up an impressive fleet of windjammers at scrap prices after the end of the First World War, the age of commercial sail would have died much earlier .

The ships Viking, Passat, and Pamir carried essential cargoes of grain from South Australia to a hungry Europe in 1949 after the Second World War. The latter two ships made the last ever rounding of the infamous Cape Horn by commercial sailing ships. Images and video footage of these later voyages give a more dramatic understanding of the perils associated with rounding Cape Horn.

The Windjammer Garthsnaid off of Cape Horn
Image courtesy of State Library of Queensland

The video website YouTube, have several interviews and inspiring film footage of "The Last Cape Horners", who sailed on these windjammers at the end of an era. The footage shows how perilous the passage round Cape Horn was, with it's extremes of weather which claimed the lives of many sailors, and sent once beautiful ships to the ocean floor.

James Later Life

The census of 1901 is the first to document his family after the voyages we have documented, it records James age 43, Agnes age 35, and their eight children living at 1 Hanover Lane, in Aberdeen. The ninth child was born after the date of the census.

James	age 16	Shipyard Labourer
William	age 14	Butchers Message Boy
Alexander	age 12	Butchers Message Boy
Agnes	age 10	Scholar
George	age 7	Scholar
Williamina	age 5	Scholar
Mary Ann	age 4	
Jane	age 2	
Alexina	age 0	

By the time the 1911 census took place James was age 52, living at 55 Wales Street, before moving to 51 Lodge Walk some time before 1918, the date recorded in Mary Ann's marriage certificate. He lived there till his death in 1937.

The First World War took its toll on the family; first Williamina who married James Hislop in June 1915, he died in the trenches of influenza, in March 1916. Their daughter Williamina died aged four months, in October 1916.

Agnes, Williamina, and Baby Williamina

Next to give their lives, were sons William who enlisted in the Gordon Highlanders in 1914, and died in July 1918, and George who enlisted in the Royal Navy Reserves, in 1914, and died a few months after his brother in September 1918. Both must have been severely injured, as they were discharged from military service, and died at home.

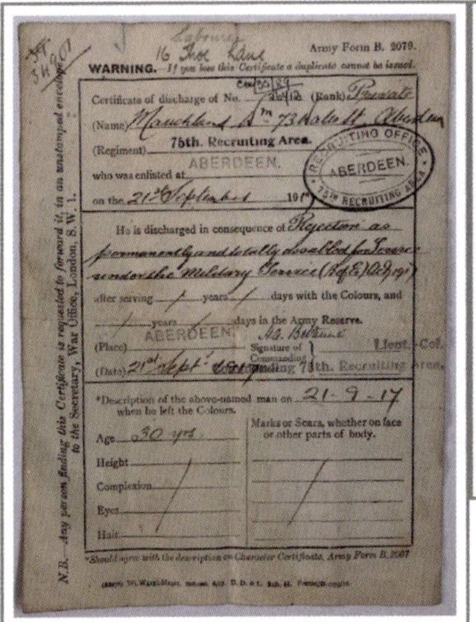

Army Form B. 2079.

WARNING.—*If you lose this Certificate a duplicate cannot be issued.*

Certificate of discharge of No. (Rank) Private

(Name) Mauchland

(Regiment) 75th. Recruiting Area.

who was enlisted at ABERDEEN.

on the 21st September 191

RECRUITING OFFICE ABERDEEN. 75th RECRUITING AREA

He is discharged in consequence of

after serving years days with the Colours, and years days in the Army Reserve.

(Place) ABERDEEN.

Signature of Commanding Lieut.-Col. 75th. Recruiting Area.

(Date) 21st Sept.

*Description of the above-named man on 21-9-17 when he left the Colours.

Age 30 yrs

Height

Complexion

Eyes

Hair

Marks or Scars, whether on face or other parts of body.

*Should agree with the description on Character Certificate, Army Form B. 2067

N.B.—Any person finding this Certificate is requested to forward it, in an unstamped envelope, to the Secretary, War Office, London, S.W. 1.

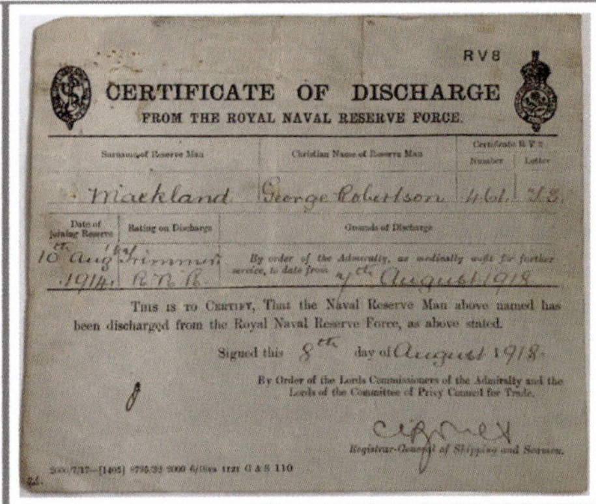

RV8

CERTIFICATE OF DISCHARGE

FROM THE ROYAL NAVAL RESERVE FORCE.

Surname of Reserve Man	Christian Name of Reserve Man	Certificate R.V. 2 Number	Letter
Mackland	George Robertson		

Date of Joining Reserve	Rating on Discharge	Grounds of Discharge
10th Aug 1914	R.N.R.	By order of the Admiralty, as medically unfit for further service, to date from 7th August 1918

This is to Certify, That the Naval Reserve Man above named has been discharged from the Royal Naval Reserve Force, as above stated.

Signed this 8th day of August 1918.

By Order of the Lords Commissioners of the Admiralty and the Lords of the Committee of Privy Council for Trade.

Registrar-General of Shipping and Seamen.

Discharge Papers

Williamina posted this rather touching notice in the news paper, in loving memory of her daughter "Wee Cuddels", also detailing the deaths of her two brothers.

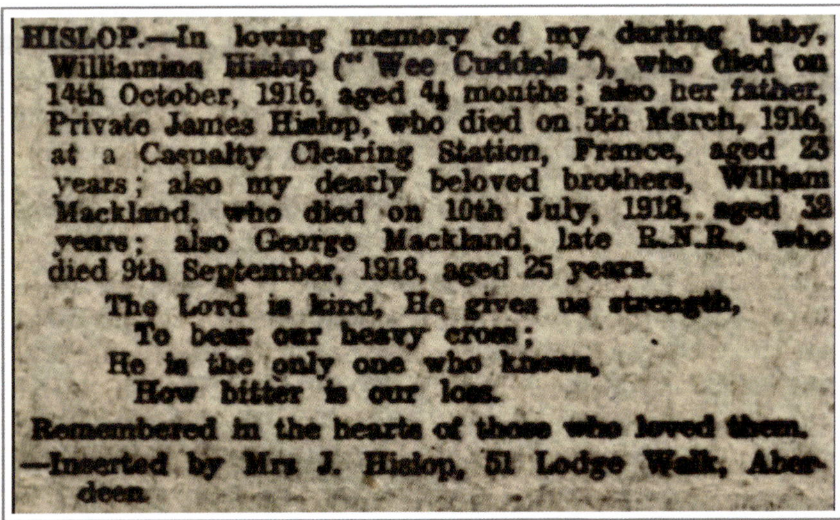

HISLOP.—In loving memory of my darling baby, Williamina Hislop ("Wee Cuddels"), who died on 14th October, 1916, aged 4½ months; also her father, Private James Hislop, who died on 5th March, 1916, at a Casualty Clearing Station, France, aged 23 years; also my dearly beloved brothers, William Mackland, who died on 10th July, 1918, aged 32 years; also George Mackland, late R.N.R., who died 9th September, 1918, aged 25 years.

The Lord is kind, He gives us strength,
To bear our heavy cross;
He is the only one who knows,
How bitter is our loss.

Remembered in the hearts of those who loved them.
—Inserted by Mrs J. Hislop, 51 Lodge Walk, Aberdeen.

James' health deteriorated in his latter years, with problems with his physical and mental health. He suffered from leg pains and knee joint failure, associated with his time at sea, this was followed by a nervous breakdown. It is not known if his Lascar pension application was successful, but we do know that he was awarded a dependants war pension linked to the death of his son George in naval service.

The war pension was originally awarded to his wife Agnus. Following her death in 1928 the pension was transferred to James. The pension amounted to 7s-2d, per week.

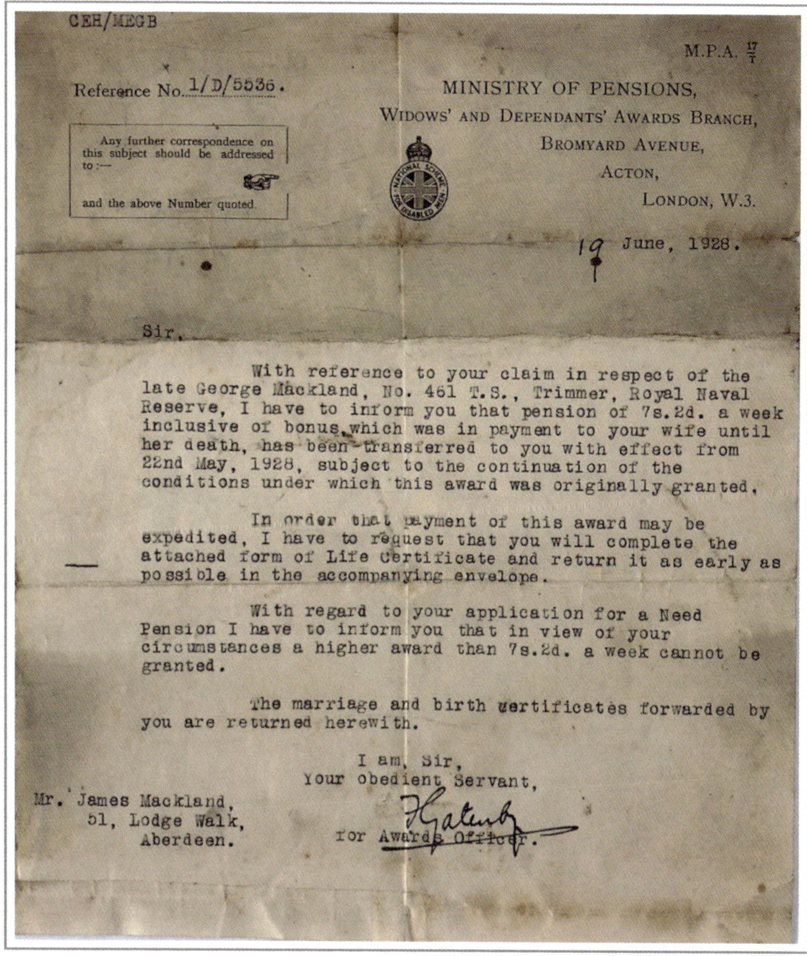

CEH/MEGB

M.P.A. 17/7

Reference No. 1/D/5536.

MINISTRY OF PENSIONS,
WIDOWS' AND DEPENDANTS' AWARDS BRANCH,
BROMYARD AVENUE,
ACTON,
LONDON, W.3.

Any further correspondence on this subject should be addressed to:— and the above Number quoted.

19 June, 1928.

Sir,

With reference to your claim in respect of the late George Mackland, No. 461 T.S., Trimmer, Royal Naval Reserve, I have to inform you that pension of 7s.2d. a week inclusive of bonus, which was in payment to your wife until her death, has been transferred to you with effect from 22nd May, 1928, subject to the continuation of the conditions under which this award was originally granted.

In order that payment of this award may be expedited, I have to request that you will complete the attached form of Life Certificate and return it as early as possible in the accompanying envelope.

With regard to your application for a Need Pension I have to inform you that in view of your circumstances a higher award than 7s.2d. a week cannot be granted.

The marriage and birth certificates forwarded by you are returned herewith.

I am, Sir,
Your obedient Servant,
[signature]
for Awards Officer.

Mr. James Mackland,
51, Lodge Walk,
Aberdeen.

James died from oesophageal cancer on 14th December 1937, aged 79. My mother recounted that in the latter stages of his cancer, he said to her that he "was seeking death". A rather sad memory for my young mother.

Agreement and Account of Crew

Brilliant 1881 - 1882 Page 1

Eng. 1.

Any Erasure, Interlineation, or Alteration in this Agreement will be void unless attested by some Superintendent of a Mercantile Marine Office, Officer of Customs, Consul, or Vice-Consul, to be made with the consent of the persons interested.

AGREEMENT No. 58903

AGREEMENT AND ACCOUNT OF CREW.

(FOREIGN-GOING SHIP.)

EXECUTED IN TWENTY PAGES.

	£	s.	d.
Engagement Fee		4	10 0
Discharging Fee		4	10 0

The term "Foreign-going Ship" means every Ship employed in trading or going between some place or places in the United Kingdom and some place or places situate beyond the following limits, that is to say, the Coasts of the United Kingdom, the Islands of Guernsey, Jersey, Sark, Alderney, and Man, and the Continent of Europe between the River Elbe and Brest inclusive.

Name of Ship.	Official No.	Port of Registry.	Port No. and Date of Register.	Registered Tonnage. Gross.	Registered Tonnage. Net.	Nominal Horse-power of Engines (if any).
"Brilliant"	77.437	Aberdeen	9/1877	1665	1613	—

REGISTERED MANAGING OWNER, or person appointed under the 38 & 39 Vict. c. 59. Name.	Address. (State No. of House, Street, and Town.)	No. of Seamen for whom accommodation is certified. (30 & 31 Vict. c. 124.)	Distance in feet and inches between centre of Maximum load line disc and upper edge of line indicating the position of the First Deck above it. ft. in.	Second Deck above it. ft. in.
John Duthie	York Place Aberdeen	50.	4. 6	- -

Scale of Provisions to be allowed and served out to the Crew during the Voyage, in addition to the daily issue of Lime and Lemon Juice and Sugar, or other antiscorbutics in any case required by Law.

	Bread lb.	Beef lb.	Pork lb.	Flour lb.	Peas pint	Rice lb.	Tea oz.	Coffee oz.	Sugar oz.	Water qts.
Sunday	1	1½	1¼	½	⅓		1/8 daily	½ do	2 weekly	3 daily
Monday	1									
Tuesday	1	1½		½						
Wednesday	1		1¼		⅓					
Thursday	1	1½		½						
Friday	1		1¼		⅓	½				
Saturday	1	1½								

SUBSTITUTES.

Equivalent at the Masters option.

The several Persons whose names are hereto subscribed, and whose descriptions are contained on the other side or sides, and of whom Seventeen are engaged as Sailors, hereby agree to serve on board the said Ship, in the several capacities expressed against their respective Names, on a Voyage from [1]

London to Sydney and any port or ports in Australia, India, China, Pacific or Atlantic Oceans, West Indies or America, trading backwards and forwards until her return to a final port of discharge in the United Kingdom. Voyage not to exceed two years.

And the Crew agree to conduct themselves in an orderly, faithful, honest, and sober manner, and to be at all times diligent in their respective Duties, and to be obedient to the lawful Commands of the said Master, or of any Person who shall lawfully succeed him, and of their Superior Officers, in every thing relating to the said Ship and the Stores and Cargo thereof, whether on board, in boats, or on shore: in consideration of which Services to be duly performed, the said Master hereby agrees to pay to the said Crew as Wages the Sums against their Names respectively expressed, and to supply them with Provisions according to the above Scale: And it is hereby agreed, That any Embezzlement or wilful or negligent Destruction of any part of the Ship's Cargo or Stores shall be made good to the Owner out of the Wages of the Person guilty of the same: And if any Person enters himself as qualified for a duty which he proves incompetent to perform, his Wages shall be reduced in proportion to his incompetency: And it is also agreed, That the Regulations authorised by the Board of Trade, which are printed herein, and numbered [2] 1 to 12 inclusive. are adopted by the parties hereto, and shall be considered as embodied in this Agreement: And it is also agreed, That if any Member of the Crew considers himself to be aggrieved by any breach of the Agreement or otherwise, he shall represent the same to the Master or Officer in charge of the Ship in a quiet and orderly manner, who shall thereupon take such steps as the case may require: And it is also agreed, That [3]

No money advanced abroad.

Wearing a knife without a laniard forfeit two days pay. Any man not joining the Ship at the appointed time substitute will be engaged

[4] The authority of the Owner or Agent for the allotments mentioned within is in my possession.

[illegible] { Superintendent, Officer of Customs, or Consular Officer.

[4] This is to be signed if such an authority has been produced, and to be scored across in ink if it has not.

In Witness whereof the said parties have subscribed their Names on the other Side or Sides hereof on the days against their respective Signatures mentioned.

Signed by [signature] Master, on the 20th day of June 1881.

These Columns to be filled up at the end of the Voyage.

Date of Commencement of Voyage.	Port at which Voyage commenced.	Date of Termination of Voyage.	Port at which Voyage terminated.	Date of Delivery of Lists to Superintendent.	I hereby declare to the truth of the Entries in this Agreement and Account of Crew, &c.
20/6/81	London	17/8/82	London	18/8/82	[signature] Master.

[1] Here the Voyage is to be described, and the places named at which the Ship is to touch, or, if that cannot be done, the general nature and probable length of the Voyage is to be stated.
[2] Here are to be inserted the numbers of any of the Regulations for preserving Discipline issued by the Board of Trade and printed on the last page hereof which the parties agree to adopt.
[3] Here any other stipulations may be inserted to which the parties agree, and which are not contrary to Law.

N.B.—This Form must not be unstitched. No leaves may be taken out of it, and none may be added or substituted. Care should be taken at the Time of Engagement that a sufficiently large Form is used. If more men are engaged during the Voyage than the number for whom signatures are provided in this Form, an additional Form Eng. 1. should be obtained and used.

[Twenty Pages.]

Brilliant 1881 - 1882 Page 2

2 **Name of Ship**

PARTICULARS OF ENGAGEMENT.

Reference No.	SIGNATURES OF CREW. (1)	Age. (2)	Town or County where born. (3)	If in the Reserve, No. of Commission or R.V.2. (4)	Ship in which he last served. State Name, and Official No. or Port she belonged to. (5)	Year. (6)	Date and Place of joining this Ship. Date. (7)	Place. (8)	In what Capacity engaged, and if Master, Mate, or Engineer, No. of his Certificate. (9)	Time at which he is to be on board. (10)
1	[illegible] (Master to sign first.)	1847	Edinburgh		Brilliant	1881			Master 87.214	
2	John Leitch	1858	Glasgow		do		1st June 1881	London	1st Mate 01494	Saturday 2nd July 1881 Noon
3	Ernest T. V. Fox	1858	Derby		Cynisca				2 Mate 08231	
4	John Farrin	1861	Aberdeen		First Ship (Allahabad)				Carpenter	
5	Thomas Carter	1836	Gosport		Allahabad	1880			Bosun	
6	James Macklan	1859	Aberdeen		First Ship				Sailmaker	
7	Henry James Apps	1840	Worcester		Brilliant	1881			Steward	
8	John Wm McCaffrey	1845	Dundee		Susan Raine				Cook	
9	John Blair	1859	Mayfair 1082 2nd C.		Cornland				AB	
10	Frederick Greenway	1860	Falmouth		Eliz. Martin				AB	
11	John McEvie	1840	Liverpool		Penthinks				AB	
12	James Henderson	1836	Shetland		Gladstone L'pool				AB	
13	John Taylor	1855	Devon		Cairnbulg Sydney				AB	
14	Roger Pertwee	1862	Chelmsford		Bride				AB	
15	William Quilty	18[illegible]	Dundee		Director Ldn				AB	
16	William Walsh	1860	Dublin		Complete St. Jno. N.B.				AB	
17	Joseph Seymour	1857	Dublin		Complete L'pool				AB	
18	Richard Algar	1857	London		Wolmsdale	1879			AB	
19	Thomas Blackwell	1853	London		Mallenny	1881			AB	
20	Peter Harris	1853	Dublin		Loches L'pool Dundee				AB	

* If any Member of the Crew enters Her Majesty's Service, the Name of the Queen's Ship into which he enters is to be stated under the head of "Cause of leaving

Ship "Brilliant"

30 June 82 AGREEMENT No. 58903 **3**

Time which he is to be on board.	Amount of Wages per Calendar Month, or Voyage	Amount of Wages advanced on Entry	Amount of Monthly Allotment	Signature or Initials of Superintendent, Consul, or Officer of Customs	PARTICULARS OF DISCHARGE, &c. (To be filled in by the Master upon the Discharge, Death, or Desertion of any Member of his Crew.) Date, Place, and Cause of leaving this Ship, or of Death. — Date	Place	Cause.*	Balance of Wages paid on Discharge	RELEASE. We, the undersigned Members of the Crew of this Ship, do hereby release this Ship, and the Master and Owner or Owners thereof, from all Claims for Wages or otherwise in respect of this Voyage. Signatures of Crew (each to be on the Line on which he signed in Col. 1).	Signature or Initials of Superintendent, Consul, or Officer of Customs before whom the Balance of Wages was paid and Release signed	Reference No.
10	£ s d	£ s d	£ s d	14	15	16	17	18	19	20	
				[illegible]	7/5/82	London	Remain			[illegible]	1
	9 9			[illegible]	do	do	do	[illegible]	John Leitch	[illegible]	2
	5 10	5 10		[illegible]	do	do	do	26 8 1	Ernest F. V. Fox	[illegible]	3
	4		2	[illegible]	do	do	do	21 7 0	John Gavin	[illegible]	4
	4 10	4 10	2 5	[illegible]	do	do	do	22 0 6	Thomas Carter	[illegible]	5
	3 15		1 17 6	[illegible]	do	do	do	10 2 6	James Macklond	[illegible]	6
	5 15	5 15	3 10	[illegible]	do	do	do	20 2 6	H. J. Apps	[illegible]	
	4 15	4 15		[illegible]	4/11/81	Sydney	Des	Sh	John Wm Coffey	[illegible]	8
	2 10	2 10		[illegible]	6/10/81	Sydney	Des	Sh	John Blair	[illegible]	9
	2 10	2 10		[illegible]	"	"	—	Sh	Frederick Greenway	[illegible]	10
	2 10	2 10		[illegible]	12/10/81	"	"	Sh	[illegible]	[illegible]	11
	2 10	2 10		[illegible]	6/10/81	Sydney	Des	Sh	James Henderson	[illegible]	12
	2 10	2 10		[illegible]	"	"	"	Sh	John Taylor	[illegible]	13
	2 10	2 10		[illegible]	"	"	"	Sh	Roger Parker	[illegible]	14
	2 10	2 10		[illegible]	"	"	"		Michael Elgar	[illegible]	15
	2 10	2 10		[illegible]	"	"	"	Sh	William Wade	[illegible]	16
	2 10	2 10		[illegible]	6/10/81	"	"	Sh	Frank R. Seymour	[illegible]	17
	2 10	2 10		[illegible]	6/10/81	Sydney	Des	Sh	Richard Elgar	[illegible]	18
	2 10	2 10		[illegible]	"	"	"	Sh	J Blackwell	[illegible]	19
	2 10	2 10		[illegible]	6/10/81	Sydney	Des	Sh	Peter Hansen	[illegible]	20

* ...the Ship," thus "H.M.S. Revenge;" and the other Causes of leaving the Ship should be briefly stated thus, "Discharged," "Deserted," "Left Sick," "Died."

[Twenty Pages.]

4 — Name of Sh[ip]

PARTICULARS OF ENGAGEMENT.

Reference No.	SIGNATURES OF CREW.	Year Born	Town or County where born.	If in the Reserve, No. of Commission or R V 2.	Ship in which he last served. State Name, and Official No. or Port she belonged to.	Year.	Date and Place of joining this Ship. Date.	Place.	In what Capacity engaged, and if Master Mate, or Engineer, No. of his Certificate	Time at which he is to be on board.
1	2	3	4	5		6	7	8	9	10
1	James Purchase	1853	London		Mary Harry	1881	1st June 1881	London	AB	Noon Saturday 2nd July /81
2	Thomas Whitehorn	1858	London		Cambrian Princess				AB	
3	William Rose	1856	Liverpool		Roderick Dhu				AB	
4	Fredrick Johnson	1853	Finland		Eliz. Marton				AB	
5	J. Peter Petersen	1854	Sweden		Bk Empire				AB	
6	Michael Sheehan	1865	London		Exmouth L'pool				Boy	
7	Thomas Apted	1865	London		do Trg Ship do				Boy	
8	Charles Brown his + mark	1840	Sweden		Pongola				AB	
9	George Page	28	Dover		Boyne L'don	do	3/7/81	Gravesend	O.S.	at once
10	Frederick Jameson	17	Kirkcaldy		H.M.S. Worcester		3.7.81	do	O.S.	do
11	James N Stewart	16	L'don		First Ship		3.7.81	do	assist Steward	do
12	William [illegible]	41	London		[illegible]	7/11/81	13/4/82	Sydney	AB	[illegible]
13	Charles Mason	28	Cornwall		[illegible]	11/1/82	13/4/82	do	AB	do
14	Luke Love	40	do		[illegible]	11/4/82	13/4/82	do	AB	do
15	Jas [illegible]	23	Sussex		Summer Rose	11/1/82	13/4/82	do	AB	do
16	John Billow	31	[illegible]		Aurora	10/1/82	13/4/82	do	AB	do
17	William Cliff	26	London		Irene	13/1/82	13/4/82	do	AB	do
18	Charles Holland	26	Plymouth		Guy Mannering	4/3/82	13/4/82	do	AB	do
19	E.P. [illegible]	34	[illegible]		[illegible]	6/3/82	13/4/82	do	AB	do
20	V Eilersen	43	Denmark		[illegible]	31/3/82	13/4/82	do	AB	do
21	Daniel [illegible]	40	London		Brilliant	31/3/82	13/4/82	do	Cook	do

* The necessary figure

† If any Member of the Crew enters Her Majesty's Service, the Name of the Queen's Ship into which he enters is to be stated under the head of "Cause of leaving

Amount of Wages per Week, Calendar Month, Share, or Voyage	Amount of Wages advanced on Entry	Amount of Weekly or Monthly Allotment	Signature or Initials of Superintendent, Consul, or Officer of Customs	PARTICULARS OF DISCHARGE, &c. To be filled in by the Master upon the Discharge, Death, or Desertion of any Member of his Crew. Date, Place, and Cause of leaving this Ship, or of Death. Date	Place	Cause†	Balance of Wages paid on Discharge	RELEASE (note M). We, the undersigned Members of the Crew of this Ship, do hereby release this Ship, and the Master and Owner or Owners thereof, from all Claims for Wages or otherwise in respect of this Voyage. Signatures of Crew (each to be on the Line on which he signed in Col. 1).	Signature or Initials of Superintendent, Consul, or Officer of Customs before whom the Balance of Wages was paid and Release signed.	Reference No.
£ s d	£ s d	13	14	15	16	17	18	19	20	
× 2 10	2 10		[illegible]	[illegible]	Sydney	[illegible]		[illegible]	[illegible]	1
× 2 10	2 10		[illegible]	"	"	[illegible]		Thomas [illegible]	[illegible]	2
× 2 10	2 10		[illegible]	Never Joined Repd on Eng 2.					L. Bone	3
× 2 10	2 10		[illegible]	[illegible]	Sydney	[illegible]		F. Johnson	[illegible]	4
× 1 1	[illegible] after the Ship arrived in Sydney		[illegible]	[illegible]	Sydney	[illegible]	3 . 4	[illegible] Peterson	[illegible]	5
1 -15	-15		[illegible]	17/8/82	London	do	8 15 6	M Sheehan	[illegible]	6
1 -15			[illegible]	do	do	do [illegible]	9 9	Thos Apted 85944	[illegible]	7
× 2 10	2 10		[illegible]	[illegible]/81	Sydney	Dischd	8 [illegible]	Charles Brown 85960 [illegible] 25/4/82	[illegible]	8
× 2 10	2 10		L. Bone	[illegible]	Sydney	[illegible]		Geo Page	[illegible]	9
1			L. B.	17/8/82	London	do				0
1			L. B. ×	[illegible]/10/81	Sydney	deserted				1
1 15	[illegible]		[illegible]	16/2/82	Newcastle	dis	1 13 0	William King	[illegible]	2
1 15			[illegible]	"	"	do	1 13 0	Charles [illegible]	[illegible]	3
1 15			[illegible]	"	"	do	1 13 0	Luke Love	[illegible]	4
1 15			[illegible]	"	"	do	1 13 0	Jas Boswell	[illegible]	5
1 15			[illegible]	"	"	do	1 13 0	John [illegible]	[illegible]	6
1 15			[illegible]	"	"	do	1 13 0	William Oliff	[illegible]	7
1 15			[illegible]	"	"	do	1 13 0	Charles Hallam	[illegible]	8
1 15			[illegible]	"	"	do	1 13 0	E. P. Howsmith	[illegible]	9
1 15			[illegible]	"	"	do	1 13 0	V Eilersen	[illegible]	0
1 15			[illegible]	"	"	do	1 15 0	Daniel Davis	[illegible]	

should be written in here.
the Ship," thus "H.M.S. Revenge;" and the other Causes of leaving the Ship should be briefly stated thus, "Discharged," "Deserted," "Left Sick," "Died."

× omitted to be endorsed by the authorities [illegible]

[Fourty Pages.]

Brilliant 1881 - 1882 Page 6

PARTICULARS OF ENGAGEMENT.

Reference No.	SIGNATURES OF CREW.	Age.	Town or County where born.	If in the Reserve, No. of Commission or R V 3.	Ship in which he last served. State Name, and Official No. or Port she belonged to.	Year.	Date and Place of joining this Ship. Date.	Place.	In what Capacity engaged, and if Master, Mate, or Engineer, No. of his Certificate.	Time at which he is to be on board.
1	2	3	4	5	6	7	8	9	10	
*1	Daniel Davis	40	London		"Brilliant"	1882	2/2/82	Newcastle	Cook	18/2/82
2	Thomas Freeman	23	Nottingham		Cambuly	17/9/81	1/3/82	Sydney	AB	
3	John McLaren	27	London		Thompson	Aug 81	1/3/82	do	AB	
4	Arch his mark McDonall.	26	Prince Ed. Island		Fiona	Jany 82	1/3/82	do	AB	
5	John Kalfrom	22	London		[illegible]	Sept 81	1/3/82	do	AB	
6	Sam Harris	24	Kingston		[illegible]	Sept 81	1/3/82	do	AB	
7	Alex Stewart	22	Glasgow		"Fiona"	182	2/3/82	Newcastle	AB	[illegible]
8	Charles Stewart	48	Greenock		Romeo	.	do	do	AB	.
9	J R Reeve	23	London		Star of Greece	.	do	do	AB	.
0	Alfred Spencer	35	London		Duke of Westminster	.	do	do	AB	.
1	John his mark Halloway	42	[illegible]		Moravian	.	do	do	AB	.
2	Charles his mark Bradford	27	Antigua		Lismore	.	do	do	AB	.
3	C F King	30	London		Shore Line	.	do	do	Deck Hand	.
4	A C Elvins	24	London		do	.	do	do	Deck Hand	.
5	R. Terry	22	Antigua		Moravian	.	do	do	AB	.
6	Geo Groves	20	Jamaica		do	.	do	do	AB	.
7	W Dunn	29	Folkstone		Potosi (S)	.	3 do	do	AB	.
8	Henry Roberts	26	London		Potosi (S)	.	do	do	AB	.
9	John Sinclair	22	Edinburgh		Neptune	.	do	do	AB	.
0	John D. S. Phillips	16	Sydney		First Ship	.	3 do	do	O.S.	.

* The necessary figure

† If any Member of the Crew enters Her Majesty's Service, the Name of the Queen's Ship into which he enters is to be stated under the head of " *Cause of leaving*

Brilliant 1881 - 1882 Page 7

Brilliant.

AGREEMENT No. 58903 **7**

Amount of Wages per Week, Calendar Month, Share, or Voyage. (11)	Amount of Wages advanced on Entry. (12)	Amount of Weekly or Monthly Allotment. (13)	Signature or Initials of Superintendent, Consul, or Officer of Customs. (14)	PARTICULARS OF DISCHARGE, &c. To be filled in by the Master upon the Discharge, Death, or Desertion of any Member of his Crew. Date, Place, and Cause of leaving this Ship, or of Death. — Date. (15)	Place. (16)	Cause.† (17)	Balance of Wages paid on Discharge. (18)	RELEASE (see M). We, the undersigned Members of the Crew of this Ship, do hereby release this Ship, and the Master and Owner or Owners thereof, from all Claims for Wages or otherwise in respect of this Voyage. Signatures of Crew (each to be on the Line on which he signed in Col. 1). (19)	Signature or Initials of Superintendent, Consul, or Officer of Customs before whom the Balance of Wages was paid and Release signed. (20)	Reference No.
6 0 0	6 0 0	. .	[illegible]	17/8/82	London	dis	[illegible]	David Davie	[illegible]	1
5 . .	5 . .		[illegible]	[illegible]	Lyttelton	NZ	Nil	95966 - 2. 3. 4. 5. J Freeman	[illegible]	2
5 . .	5 . .		[illegible]	17/8/82	London	dis	17.10.4	John Maclaren	[illegible]	3
5 . .	5 . .		[illegible]	do	do	do	18.1.6	95978.79 Archd McDougall his mark	[illegible]	4
5 . .	5 . .		[illegible]	Did not Join				95975.6.7		5
5 . .	5 . .		[illegible]	17/8/82	London	dis	19.0.2	Sam Harris	[illegible]	6
5 . .	5 . .		[illegible]	29/3/82	Lyttelton	Deserted NZ		95972.3.4	[illegible]	7
5 . .	5 . .		[illegible]	17/8/82	London	dis	[illegible]	Charles Sherman	[illegible]	8
5 . .	5 . .		[illegible]	do	do	do	18.11.11	95969.70.71 J R Reeve	[illegible]	9
5 . .	5 . .		[illegible]	do	do	do	17.2.1	Alfred Spencer 95986	[illegible]	0
5 . .	5 . .		[illegible]	29/3/82	Lyttelton	Deserted			[illegible]	1
5 . .	5 . .		[illegible]	17/8/82	London	dis	19.7.4	Chas Bradford his mark	[illegible]	2
1 . .	. .		[illegible]	23/3/82	Lyttelton	NZ	Nil	95991.2.3 C J King	[illegible]	3
1 . .	. .		[illegible]	"	"	"	Nil	A McElvine	[illegible]	4
5 . .	5 . .		[illegible]	17/8/82	London	dis	19.5.4	R Jerry	[illegible]	5
5 . .	5 . .		[illegible]	do	do	do	19.7.4	95987.8.3 R Grover	[illegible]	6
5 . .	2 10 .	Further sum to Lyttelton	[illegible]	23/3/82	Lyttelton	NZ	2.10	95987.8 W Turner	[illegible]	7
5 . .	. . .	Same Terms	[illegible]	23/3/82	"	NZ	5 10 0	Henry Roberts	[illegible]	8
5 . .	2 10 0	Same Terms	[illegible]	"	"	"	2.10	John Sinclair	[illegible]	9
1 . .	. .		[illegible]	17/8/82	London	dis	4.1.6	John D S Phillips	[illegible]	0

should be written in here. the Ship," thus "H.M.S. Revenge;" and the other Causes of leaving the Ship should be briefly stated thus, "Discharged," "Deserted," "Left Sick," "Died."

[Twenty Payers.]

Brilliant 1881 - 1882 Page 8

8 **Name of Ship**

PARTICULARS OF ENGAGEMENT.

Reference No.	SIGNATURES OF CREW	Age.	Town or County where born.	If in the Reserve, No. of Commission or R V 2.	Ship in which he last served. State Name, and Official No. or Port she belonged to.	Year.	Date and Place of joining this Ship. Date.	Place.	In what Capacity engaged, and if Master, Mate, or Engineer, No. of his Certificate.	Time at which he is to be on board	Amount of Wages per Week, Calendar Month, Share, or Voyage.
1	2	3	4	5	6	7	8	9	10	11	
*1	Wm. his mark Robertson	25	Perth	5.5.82 Lyttelton	[illegible] of Wellington	1882	10th May	Lyttelton	AB	6 am 12.5	7
2	Donald Corsie	29	Kirkcudbright?	1879 [illegible]	[illegible] of Shields	"	"	"	AB	"	7
3	John Nelson	22	Glasgow	1882 5.5.82	Circe? of Lyttelton	"	"	"	AB	"	7
4	Frederick Holden	38	Southwick?	1878 [illegible]	Chile? of Lyttelton	"	"	"	AB	"	7
5	Edward Moore	37	London	28.5.82 [illegible]	[illegible] of Wellington	"	"	"	AB	13th	7
6	James his mark Smith	32	Portsmouth	10.4.82 Lyttelton	St Hilda of Wellington	"	"	"	AB	13th	7
7	Charles his mark Gray	40	Portland	28.4.82 Lyttelton	Esther of "	"	"	"	AB	13th	7
8	E. Gilbert	37	[illegible]	28.4.82 Lyttelton	Wigtonshire? of Glasgow	"	"	"	AB	"	7
9	W. Woodland	22	London	1882 Lyttelton	[illegible] of York	"	"	"	AB	"	7
0	F. C. Simmons	2[illegible]	London		Waikato [illegible]	75.	12th	"	2nd Steward	"	
1	[illegible]	See No. 2 above									
2											
3											
4											
5											
6											
7											
8											
9											
0											

† If any Member of the Crew enters Her Majesty's Service, the Name of the Queen's Ship into which he enters is to be stated under the head of "Cause of leaving

* The necessary figure

14 **Name of Ship**

ACCOUNT OF APPRENTICES ON BOARD (IF ANY).

Christian and Surnames of the Apprentices at full length.	Born	Registry of Indenture.		Registry of Assignment.		Date, Place, and Cause of leaving this Ship, or of Death. *To be filled up by the Master.*		
		Date of	Port of	Date of	Port of	Date.	Place.	Cause.
1	2	3	4	5	6	7	8	9
Robert William Peak Freeman	1862	1/7/79	London			Still by the Ship		
George Alexander Flower	1866	12/8/79	London				do	do
Thomas Lewis Thomas	1864	8/9/80	London				do	do
Robert James Bangard	1865	31/8/80	London				do	do
W. C. Cose	1866	7/9/80	London				do	do

PARTICULARS RELATING TO

WAGES AND EFFECTS OF SEAMEN AND APPRENTICES DECEASED DURING THE VOYAGE.

(TAKEN FROM THE OFFICIAL LOG.)

Note.—Particulars of the Moneys due to each deceased Seaman, and of his Clothes and Effects, and of Deductions (if any), are to accompany this Return in a separate Form W & E 1. (late KK.), which will be furnished by the Superintendent. If any Master fails to give a true account of these particulars, he will be liable to forfeit a sum not exceeding treble the value of the money and effects not accounted for, or to a penalty not exceeding £50.

Reference No. in Agreement.	Christian and Surname of Deceased.	Certificates, if any. Description. State whether "Mate's," "Engineer's," "Naval Reserve," &c.	Certificates, if any. Numbers.	Net Amount of Wages, and total Proceeds of Sale of Effects paid to Superintendent, Officer of Customs, or Consul, as per Account in Form W & E 1.	Particulars of Effects (if any) delivered to Superintendent, Officer of Customs, or Consul, as per Account in Form W & E 1.
1	2	3	4	5	6
		None			

Ship *Brilliant* AGREEMENT No. 58903 **15**

PARTICULARS OF ALL

MARRIAGES

THAT HAVE OCCURRED ON BOARD DURING THE VOYAGE. (TAKEN FROM THE OFFICIAL LOG.)

Note.—Section 282 of the Merchant Shipping Act, 1854, requires the Master of the Ship to enter in his Official Log the particulars of every Marriage that has taken place on board; and sections 273 and 274 require that a List of such Marriages should be made out and delivered to a Superintendent of a Mercantile Marine Office in the United Kingdom.

Date when Married. 1	Christian and Surnames of both Parties. 2	Ages. 3	State whether Single, Widow, or Widower. 4	Profession or Occupation. 5	Father's Christian and Surname. 6	Profession or Occupation of Father. 7
			None			

No Scurvy W.L. — No Stowaways W.L.

CERTIFICATES

OR INDORSEMENTS MADE BY CONSULS OR BY OFFICERS IN BRITISH POSSESSIONS ABROAD.

Engaged (10)

I hereby certify that I have sanctioned the Engagement of "William King" C. Mason Luke Rose" "James Doswell" Wm Cliff Charles Hallam" E P Herweth, & Eilersen Daniel Dans, upon the terms mentioned in the within-written agreement, that I have ascertained and am satisfied that they fully understand the said agreement and have signed the same in my presence.

[illegible]
Shipping Master

Discharged (18)

I certify that the within-named John McCaffery, John Blair F. McGreeway, John Melville, Johan Anderson, P Pertwee Wm Walsh, William Quilty, Frank Seymour Richard Algar Thos Blackwell P Masons James Purchase Thos Whitehorn, H. Johnson J. P. Petersen, Chas Brown, & George Page have been left behind at this port on the alleged ground of mutual consent, that they all forfeited their wages to get their discharge excepting J P Petersen who received £3.0.0 and Chas Brown £8.12.4 left in hospital and their effects removed from the vessel

[illegible]
Shipping Master

[Twenty Pages.]

N.B. I find that the name of Joh Saylor has been omitted from the above [illegible]

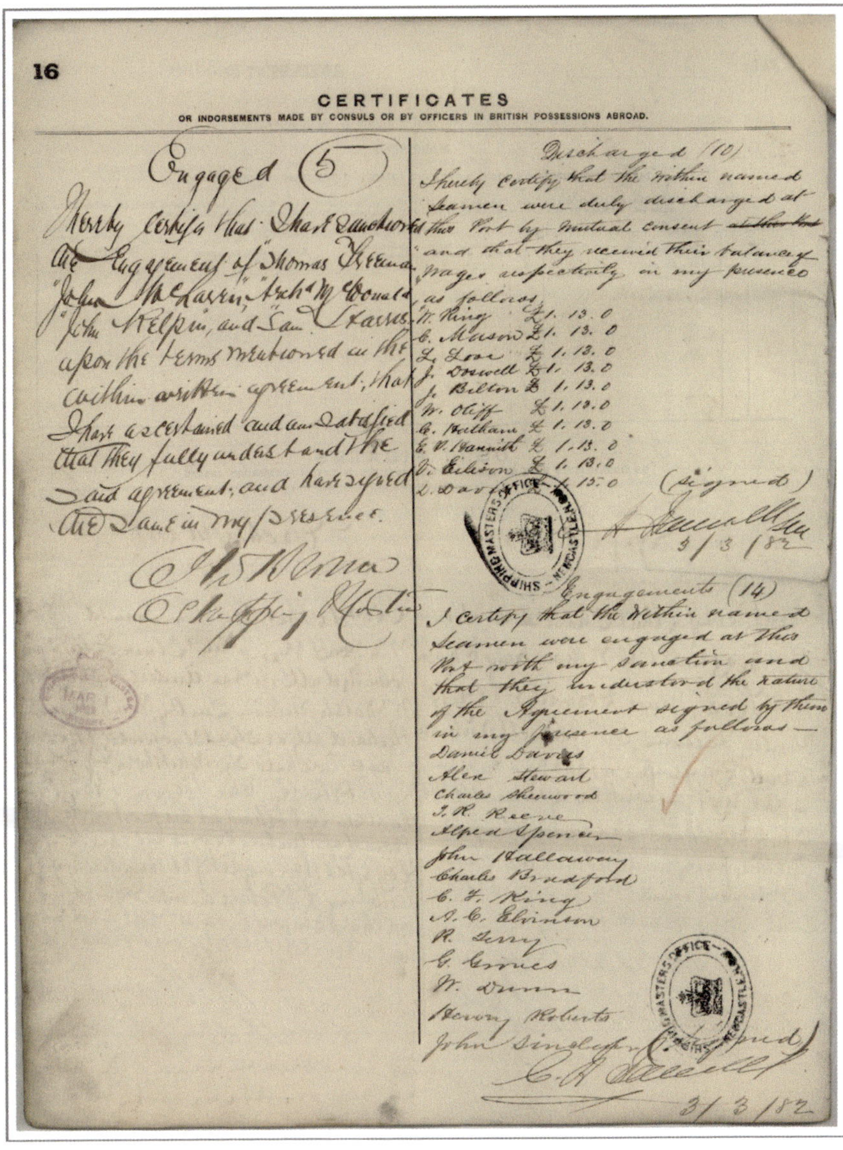

16

CERTIFICATES

OR INDORSEMENTS MADE BY CONSULS OR BY OFFICERS IN BRITISH POSSESSIONS ABROAD.

Engaged (5)

I hereby certify that I have sanctioned the Engagement of "Thomas Freeman," "John McLaren," "Archd McDonald," "John Kelpin," and "Sam Stares" upon the terms mentioned in the within written agreement; that I have ascertained and am satisfied that they fully understand the said agreement, and have signed the same in my presence.

[illegible signature]
Shipping Master

Discharged (10)

I hereby certify that the within named Seamen were duly discharged at this Port by mutual consent ~~[illegible]~~ and that they received their balance of wages respectively in my presence as follows

W. King £1. 13. 0
C. Mason £1. 13. 0
L. Love £1. 13. 0
J. Doswell £1. 13. 0
J. Bilton £1. 13. 0
W. Oliff £1. 13. 0
C. Holtham £1. 13. 0
E. V. Hannith £1. 13. 0
V. Eilison £1. 13. 0
L. Dav[illegible] £1. 15. 0

(Signed)
[illegible signature]
3/3/82

Engagements (14)

I certify that the within named Seamen were engaged at this Port with my sanction and that they understood the nature of the Agreement signed by them in my presence as follows —

Daniel Davies
Alex Stewart
Charles Sherwood
T. R. Reeve
Alfred Spencer
John Halloway
Charles Bradford
C. F. King
A. C. Elvinton
R. Terry
G. Grimes
W. Dunn
Henry Roberts
John Sinclair

(Signed)
C. H. [illegible]
3/3/82

AGREEMENT No. 58903 **17**

CERTIFICATES

OR INDORSEMENTS MADE BY CONSULS OR BY OFFICERS IN BRITISH POSSESSIONS ABROAD.

H. M. Customs
Lyttelton
12th May 1882

I hereby certify that this agreement was deposited in this office on the 28 day of March 1882 and was returned to the within named Master on the 12th day of May 1882.

A. P. Brownes Coll.

H. M. Customs
Lyttelton
12th May 1882

I hereby certify that the undermentioned Seamen were discharged and left behind at the Port of Lyttelton on the alleged ground of mutual consent that the allegation is true and that their wages have been paid to them in cash and their effects delivered to them. Thos Truman, J King, A. J. Blomes, Wm Dunn, Harry Roberts, John [illegible]

[illegible] Coll

H. M. Customs
Lyttelton
12th May 1882

I hereby certify that the undermentioned Seamen were left behind at the Port of Lyttelton on the alleged ground of desertion that the allegation is true and that a proper entry of the same made by the master in official log book has been presented to me for inspection. Alexander Stewart, John Holloway

[illegible]

H. M. Customs
Lyttelton
12th May 1882

I hereby certify that I have sanctioned the engagement of the undermentioned Seamen upon the terms of the within named agreement and that I am perfectly certain they fully understand its nature and have signed the same in my presence. Wm Robertson, Donald Currie, John Nelson, Fred Holden, E Morgan, James Smith, Chas Gray, E. Gilbert, Jno Woodland

[illegible]

[Twenty Pages.]

Eng. 1.

** Any Erasure, Interlineation, or Alteration in this Agreement will be void, unless attested by some Superintendent of a Mercantile Marine Office, Officer of Customs, Consul, or Vice-Consul, to be made with the consent of the persons interested.

Sanctioned by the Board of Trade, ... in pursuance of ... Vict. c. ...

1883

AGREEMENT AND ACCOUNT OF CREW.

FOREIGN-GOING SHIP.

EXECUTED IN SIXTEEN PAGES.

	£	s.	d.
Engagement Fee			
Discharging Fee	Nil		

The term "Foreign-going Ship" means every Ship employed in trading or going between some place or places in the United Kingdom and some place or places situate beyond the following limits, that is to say, the Coasts of the United Kingdom, the Islands of Guernsey, Jersey, Sark, Alderney, and Man, and the Continent of Europe between the River Elbe and Brest inclusive.

Name of Ship.	Official No.	Port of Registry.	Registered Tonnage. Gross.	Net.	Nominal Horse power of Engines (if any).
Brilliant	71437	Aberdeen	1665	1613	—

REGISTERED MANAGING OWNER, or person appointed under the 38 & 39 Vict. c. 88. Name.	Address. (State No. of House, Street, and Town.)	No. of Seamen for whom accommodation is certified. (30 & 31 Vict. c. 124.)	Distance in feet and inches between the centre of the Disc showing the Maximum load line in salt water and the upper edge of lines indicating the position of the Ship's decks above that centre. First Deck, above it. ft. in.	Second Deck, above it. ft. in.
Alexr. Duthie	Aberdeen	50	4 6	—

Scale of Provisions to be allowed and served out to the Crew during the Voyage, in addition to the daily issue of Lime and Lemon Juice and Sugar, or other antiscorbutics in any case required by 30th & 31st Vict., c. 124, s. 4.

	Bread lb.	Beef lb.	Pork lb.	Tinned Meats lb.	Soup and Bouilli pint.	Preserved Potatoes lb.	Compressed or Preserved Vegetables lb.	Flour lb.	Pease pint.	Rice lb.	Tea oz.	Coffee oz.	Sugar oz.	Molasses qt.	Water qt.
Sunday	1	1½	1¼					½			1/8	½	2	-	3
Monday	1								⅓						
Tuesday	1	1½													
Wednesday	1		1¼					½			Daily				
Thursday	1	1½							⅓						
Friday	1		1¼												
Saturday	1	1½						½	⅓	½					

Note.—In any case an equal quantity of Fresh Meat or Fresh Vegetables may, at the option of the Master, be served out in lieu of the Salted or Tinned Meats or Preserved or Compressed Vegetables named in the above scale.

SUBSTITUTES. NO SPIRITS ALLOWED

EQUIVALENT SUBSTITUTES AT THE MASTER'S OPTION

The several Persons whose names are hereto subscribed, and whose descriptions are contained on the other side or sides, and of whom Fifteen are engaged as Sailors, hereby agree to serve on board the said Ship, in the several capacities expressed against their respective Names, on a Voyage from [1] London to Sydney and any Port or Places in Australia, New Zealand, India, China, Pacific and Atlantic Oceans, West Indies and America, trading backwards and forwards, as the Master may require, until the return of the Ship to a final port of discharge in the United Kingdom, calling at a Port for orders if required. Voyage not to exceed two years. —

And the Crew agree to conduct themselves in an orderly, faithful, honest, and sober manner, and to be at all times diligent in their respective Duties, and to be obedient to the lawful Commands of the said Master, or of any Person who shall lawfully succeed him, and of their Superior Officers, in everything relating to the said Ship and the Stores and Cargo thereof, whether on board, in boats, or on shore: in consideration of which Services to be duly performed, the said Master hereby agrees to pay to the said Crew as Wages the Sums against their Names respectively expressed, and to supply them with Provisions according to the above Scale. And it is hereby agreed, That any Embezzlement or wilful or negligent Destruction of any part of the Ship's Cargo or Stores shall be made good to the Owner out of the Wages of the Person guilty of the same: And if any Person enters himself as qualified for a duty which he proves incompetent to perform, his Wages shall be reduced in proportion to his incompetency: And it is also agreed, That the Regulations authorized by the Board of Trade, which are printed herein and numbered [2] 1 to 4

are adopted by the parties hereto, and shall be considered as embodied in this Agreement: And it is also agreed, That if any Member of the Crew considers himself to be aggrieved by any breach of the Agreement or otherwise, he shall represent the same to the Master or Officer in charge of the Ship in a quiet and orderly manner, who shall thereupon take such steps as the case may require: And it is also agreed, That [3] Thirty two hands all told are to be considered the ship's full complement of Crew

[Handwritten:] carrying knife without a lanyard, on each occasion two days pay. Smoking or being in forecastle during watch on deck one days pay. Any person not on board at the time appointed a substitute will be shipped at once

[4] The authority of the Owner or Agent for the allotments mentioned within is in my possession.

W. Land Dy. Superintendent, Officer of Customs, or Consular Officer.

[4] This is to be signed if such an authority has been produced, and to be scored across in ink if it has not.

In Witness whereof the said parties have subscribed their Names on the other Side or Sides hereof on the days against their respective Signatures mentioned.

Signed by J. H. Danaldson Master,

on the Fourth day of October 1882

Date of Commencement of Voyage.	Port at which Voyage commenced.	Date of Termination of Voyage.	Port at which Voyage terminated.	Date of Delivery of Lists to Superintendent.	I hereby declare to the truth of the Entries in this Agreement and Account of Crew, &c.
M.M. Office OC 4 82		7/8/83	London	8/8/83	J. H. Danaldson

(These Columns to be filled up at the end of the Voyage.)

[1] Here the Voyage is to be described, and the places named at which the Ship is to touch, or, if that cannot be done, the general nature and probable length of the Voyage is to be stated.
[2] Here are to be inserted the numbers of any of the Regulations for preserving Discipline issued by the Board of Trade and printed on the last page hereof which the parties agree to adopt.
[3] Here any other stipulations may be inserted to which the parties agree, and which are not contrary to Law.

N.B.—This Form must not be unstitched. No leaves may be taken out of it, and none may be added or substituted. Care should be taken at the time of Engagement that a sufficiently large Form is used. If more men are engaged during the Voyage than the number for whom signatures are provided in this Form, an additional Form Eng. 1. should be obtained and used.

W.J.J. ... 1-81 ... [Sixteen Pages.]

Brilliant 1882 - 1883 Page 2

2 Name of

PARTICULARS OF ENGAGEMENT.

Reference No.	Signatures of Crew.	Year of Birth.	Town or County where born.	If in the Reserve, No. of Commission or R.V.E.	Ship in which he last served, and Year of Discharge therefrom. Year.	State Name and Official No. or Port she belonged to.	Date and Place of joining present Ship. Date.	Place.	In what Capacity engaged, and if Master, Mate, or Engineer, No. of his Certificate.	Time at which he is to be on board.
1	2	3	4	5	6	7	8	9	10	
1	[illegible] (Master to sign first)	1847	Edinboro	1882	Brilliant	Oct		Master [illegible]	
2	John Leitch	1855	Glasgow	"	do	"		1 Mate	
3	Ernest T. V. Fox	1858	Derbyshire	"	do	"		2 Mate	
4	George A Flower	1857	Ldon	"	do	"		3 Mate	
5	T Carter	1839	Portsmouth	"	do	"		1 Steward	
6	John Garin	1862	do do	"	do	"	London	Carptr	
7	James Mackland	1859	do	"	do	"		Sailmkr	
8	Henry James Apps	1831	Worcester	"	do	"		Steward	
9	Edwin Lewis	1862	Rhoin		Trainship	"		2 Steward	
10	Ath Le Burki	1843	France	1882	Cariboo	"		Cook	
11	Walter Hill	1859	Leicester	"	Lottie Whittaker Ldon	"		AB	
12	Andrew Kelly	1852	Lpool	"	Calabria New Haven	"	Office	AB	
13	H. Bjorklund	1867	Gothenburg Sweden	"	Wolseley Ldon	"		AB	
14	T. Oliver	1836	N Jdno	"	Eddiboro do	"		AB	
15	John Matthews	1845	Wellington NZ	"	Carnaquhan	"		AB	
16	J. Petrovitch his x mark	1834	Austria	"	Whare Tone Ldon	"		AB	
17	John Mitchell	1832	Kirkcaldy	"	Irrawaddy Dundee	"		AB	
18	John Randa	1860	Gothland	"	Loch Lomond Glow	"		AB	
19	Wm Smith his x mark	1853	Boston US	"	May Belfast do	"		AB	
20	Bo Flaherty his x mark	1843	Galway	"	Persian Empire Ldon	"		AB	

Saturday - 7 October 1882 - 6am

* If any Member of the Crew enters Her Majesty's Service, the Name of the Queen's Ship into which he enters is to be stated under the head of "Cause of Leaving

Ship Brilliant 67451 to 67461/5 97/n 28/5/83 (40402 to 67461/5 40450/5 28/5/83 97/n) 3

Amount of Wages per Calendar Month, or Voyage (11)	Amount of Wages advanced on Entry (12)	Amount of Monthly Allotment (13)	Signature or Initials of Superintendent, Consul, or Officer of Customs (14)	PARTICULARS OF DISCHARGE, &c. To be filled in by the Master upon the Discharge, Death, or Desertion of any Member of his Crew. Date, Place and Cause of leaving this Ship, or of Death. Date (15)	Place (16)	Cause.* (17)	Balance of Wages paid on Discharge (18)	RELEASE (Sale M). We, the undersigned Members of the Crew of this Ship, do hereby release this Ship and the Master and Owner or Owners thereof, from all Claims for Wages, or otherwise in respect of this Voyage. Signatures of Crew (each to be on the Line on which he signed in Col. 1). (19)	Signature or Initials of Superintendent, Consul, or Officer of Customs before whom the Balance of Wages was paid and Release signed. (20)	Reference No.
			W. McCaudry	Remains						1
9	Lor Pay 1 Mth	4 6	MB	7/8/83	L'don	Dischd	35 14 10	John Leitch	TWB	2
5. 15.	Mo do	2 17 6	MB	do	do	do	26 10 9	Ernest W. Fox	TWB	3
11 0. 0			MB	do	do	do	—	George A. Flower	TWB	4
4. 15.		2 15 0	MB	12/1/83	Sydney	Died	Nil	Thomas Carter	[illegible]	5
6		3	MB	7/8/83	L'don	Dischd	21 0 0	John Garran	TWB	6
4. 10. 0		2. 5.	MB	do	do	do	8 18 0	James Maitland	TWB	7
5. 5.		3. 15.	MB	do	do	do	18 13 4	Henry James App	TWB	8
1			MB	5/1/83	Sydney	Dis	Nil	Edwin Lewis	[illegible]	9
10	for run to be discharged at Sydney		MB	5/1/83	do	do	10 0 0	Th. Le Barb	[illegible]	10
3	two days after ship is moored at wharf; Lor Pay 1 Mth	1. 10. 0	MB	8/1/83	do	do	Nil	Walter Hill	[illegible]	11
3	do	1. 10. 0	MB	8/1/83	do	do	Nil	Andrew Kelly	[illegible]	12
3	do	1. 10. 0	MB	11/1/83	do	Deserted			[illegible]	13
3	do	1. 10. 0	MB	11/1/83	Sydney	Dis Nil		F. Oliver	[illegible]	14
3	do	1. 10. 0	MB	8/1/83	do	do	Nil	John Mather	[illegible]	15
3	do	1. 10. 0	MB	7/8/83	L'don	Dischd	19 17 0	D. Petrovich his X mark	TWB	16
3	do	1. 10. 0	MB	8/1/83	Sydney	Dis	Nil	[illegible]	[illegible]	17
3	do	1. 10. 0	MB	7/1/83	do	Deserted			[illegible]	18
3	do	1. 10. 0	MB	11/1/83	do	do			[illegible]	19
3	do	1. 10. 0	MB	8/1/83	Sydney	Dis	Nil	P. B. X O'Hanty	[illegible]	20

*the Ship, thus "H.M.S. Revenge," and the other Causes of leaving the Ship should be briefly stated thus, "Discharged," "Deserted," "Left Sick," "Died."

[Sixteen Pages.]

Brilliant 1882 - 1883 Page 4

4 **Name of**

PARTICULARS OF ENGAGEMENT.

Reference No.	SIGNATURES OF CREW.	Year of Birth.	Town or County where born.	If in the Reserve, No. of Commission or R V 2.	Ship in which he last served, and Year of Discharge therefrom. Year.	State Name, and Official No. or Port she belonged to.	Date and Place of joining present Ship. Date.	Place.	In what Capacity engaged, and if Master, Mate, or Engineer, No. of his Certificate.	Time at which he is to be on board.
	1	2	3	4	5	6	7	8	9	10
21	James Lawrence	1862	Portsmouth		1882	San Lorenzo	4 Oct	London	AB	7 [illegible]
22	Henry Calvard	1859	Ldon		"	Dumbritton Glasgow	"	"	AB	"
23	John Warden	1854	Lundd		"	Carnarvonshire	"	"	AB	"
24	J. Gordon	1844	Morvados		"	Aviemore Ldon	"	"	AB	"
25	Albert Sterns	1857	Ldon		"	Guy Mannering Ab dn	"	"	AB	"
26	Arthur Carter	1860	W Cowes	134476	"	Ermabrudah Glasgow	"	"	AB	"
27	Chas Olsen	1841	Fredrikstad		"	Carnarvonshire Ldon	"	"	AB	"
28	A Adnodt	1833	Farsund Norway		"	Norwegian ship	"	"	AB Quartermaster	"
29	Thos Apted	1865	Ldon		"	Brilliant	"	"	OS	"
30	Michael Sheehan	1865	do		"	do	"	"	OS	"
31	Walter Cottam	1859	Bossedon			First Ship	"	"	Groom for Horses	
32	Isaac Franks	25	Birmingham			Monterey	2/4/83	Sydney	[illegible]	4th [illegible]
33	Chas Mackintosh	34	London		"	La Vague	5/4/83	do	[illegible]	do
34	[illegible] Thomas	27	France			[illegible]	9/4/83	do	AB	do
35	Wm Robinson	1846	Birmingham			Brilliant	9/4/83	do	AB	[illegible]
36	F Williams	19	Victoria			Shore Service	9/4/83	do	OS	11th [illegible]
37	Walter Grant	39	Scotland			[illegible]	11/4/83	do	AB	[illegible]
38	Andrew Golden	33	York			Shore Service	11/4/83	do	OS	[illegible]
39	George Mourant	27	Jersey			[illegible]	11/4/83	do	AB	12 [illegible]
40	John Hall	23	Manchester			Brilliant	13/4/83	do	AB	13 [illegible]

*If any Member of the Crew enters Her Majesty's Service, the Name of the Queen's Ship into which he enters is to be stated under the head of "Cause of Leaving

Brilliant 1882 - 1883 Page 5

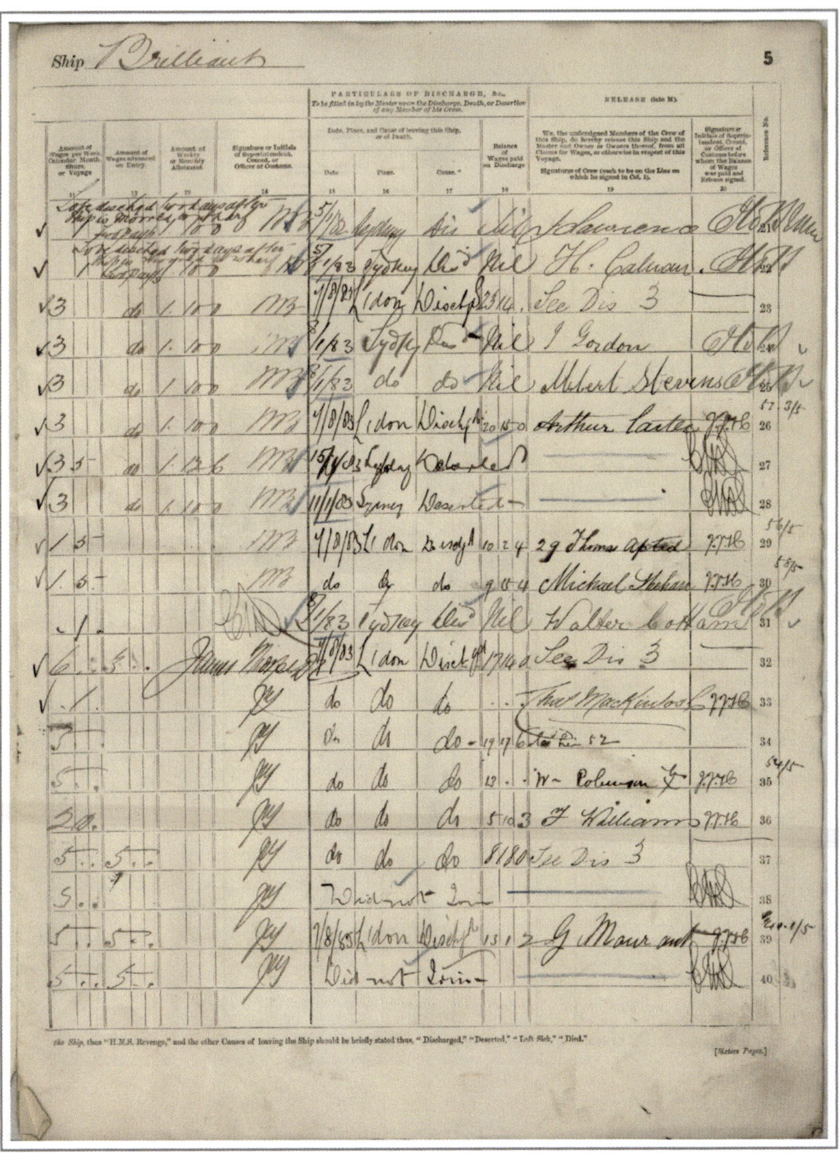

Ship Brilliant 5

Amount of Wages per Week, Calendar Month, Share, or Voyage (11)	Amount of Wages advanced on Entry (12)	Amount of Weekly or Monthly Allotment (13)	Signature or Initials of Superintendent, Consul, or Officer of Customs (14)	Date (15)	Place (16)	Cause (17)	Balance of Wages paid on Discharge (18)	Release: Signatures of Crew (19)	Signature or Initials of Superintendent, Consul, or Officer of Customs before whom the Balance of Wages was paid and Release signed (20)	Reference No.
Tobe docked two days after Ship is moored to wharf		1.10.0	MB	5/1/83	Sydney	Dis	Nil	J. Lawrence		21
1 Tobe docked two days after Ship is moored to wharf		1.10.0	MB	5/1/83	Sydney	Dis	Nil	H. Calnan		22
3	do	1.10.0	MB	7/8/83	L'don	Disch	25.14.	See Dis 3		23
3	do	1.10.0	MB	8/1/83	Sydney	Dis	Nil	J Gordon		24
3	do	1.10.0	MB	8/1/83	do	do	Nil	Albert Stevens		25
3	do	1.10.0	MB	7/8/83	L'don	Disch	20.15.0	Arthur Carter		26
3.5	do	1.12.6	MB	15/1/83	Sydney	Deserted				27
3	do	1.10.0	MB	11/1/83	Sydney	Deserted				28
1.5			MB	7/8/83	L'don	Disch	10.2.4	Thomas Apted		29
1.5			MB	do	do	do	9.0.4	Michael Sheehan		30
1				8/1/83	Sydney	Dis	Nil	Walter Cotham		31
6.5			James Morgan	7/8/83	L'don	Disch	17.14.0	See Dis 3		32
1			JY	do	do	do	..	Thos Mackintosh		33
5			JY	do	do	do	19.17.6			34
5			JY	do	do	do	12..	W. Robinson		35
2.0			JY	do	do	do	5.10.3	F Williams		36
5	5		JY	do	do	do	8.18.0	See Dis 3		37
5			JY	Did not Join						38
5	5		JY	7/8/83	L'don	Disch	13.1.2	G. Maurant		39
5	5		JY	Did not Join						40

the Ship, thus "H.M.S. Revenge," and the other Causes of leaving the Ship should be briefly stated thus, "Discharged," "Deserted," "Left Sick," "Died."

[Sixteen Pages.]

Brilliant 1882 - 1883 Page 6

6 *Name of*

PARTICULARS OF ENGAGEMENT.

Reference No.	Signatures of Crew.	Year of Birth.	Town or County where born.	If in the Reserve, No. of Commission or R V 2.	Ship in which he last served, and Year of Discharge therefrom.		Date and Place of joining present Ship.		In what Capacity engaged and if Master, Mate, or Engineer, No. of his Certificate.	Time at which he is to be on board.
					Year.	State Name, and Official No. or Port she belonged to.	Date.	Place.		
	1	2	3	4	5	6	7	8	9	10
41	Wm. his x mark George	42	Wales	"	[illegible]	13/4/83	Sydney	A.B.	13/4/83 8 am
42	Frank R. Bevan	32	London	1883	[illegible]	13/4/83	do	A.B.	14/6 am
43	Frank his x mark Keogh	41	St Johns N.B.	"	[illegible]	16/4/83	do	A.B.	17 9 am
44	Jas Rowland	27	Bell	"	[illegible]	16/4/83	do	A.B.	do
45	Alick Nicolson	28	Glasgow	"	do	16/4/83	do	A.B.	do
46	A. Smith	42	Kirkcaldy	"	do	16/4/83	do	A.B.	do
47	William Smith	31	Bristol	"	do	16/4/83	do	A.B.	do
48	John Jones	27	Carnarvon	"	Jelandia	16/4/83	Do	A B	Do.
49	John his mark Smith	32	New Jersey	"	Alexandrovna	10/4/83	Do	A B	at once
50	E. Foster	19	London	"	Liguria	15/4/83	Do	O S	Do
51	John Adams.	19	London	"	Allowrie	19/4/83	Do	Deckhand	Do
52	R. W. B. Framan	21	West Bromwich		"Brilliant"	26/6/83	At Sea	A B	27th June
53										
54										
55										
56										
57										
58										
59										
60										

* If any Member of the Crew enters Her Majesty's Service, the Name of the Queen's Ship into which he enters is to be stated under the head of " Cause of Leaving

Brilliant 1882 - 1883 Page 7

Ship "Brilliant" 7

Amount of Wages per Week, Calendar Month, Share, or Voyage (11)	Amount of Wages advanced on Entry (12)	Amount of Weekly or Monthly Allotment (13)	Signature or Initials of Superintendent, Consul, or Officer of Customs (14)	PARTICULARS OF DISCHARGE, &c. Date (15)	Place (16)	Cause.* (17)	Balance of Wages paid on Discharge (18)	RELEASE. Signatures of Crew (19)	Signatures or Initials of Superintendent, Consul, or Officer of Customs before whom the Balance of Wages was paid and Release signed (20)	Reference No.	
5 . .	5 . .		[illegible]	7/8/83	London	Disch^d	11 0 10	William George his x mark	J.J.H.C.	41	42. 7/5
5 . .	5 . .		[illegible]	Did not Join					[illegible]	42	
5 . .	5 . .		[illegible]	7/8/83	London	Disch^d	16 4 10	Frank Keogh his x mark	J.J.H.C.	43	44. 5/5
5 10 .	5 . .		[illegible]	do	do	do	12 7 6	Jas Rowland	J.J.H.C.	44	36. 7/5
5 10 .	5 . .		[illegible]	do	do	do	12 14 0	See Dis 3		45	
5 10 .	5 . .		[illegible]	do	do	do	14 4 6	See Dis 3	—	46	
5 10 .	5 . .		[illegible]	do	do	do	13 12 6	See Dis 3	—	47	
5 10 .	2 10 .		C.W. Davison	do	do	do	15 10 6	See Dis 3	—	48	
5 10 .	5 10 .		C.W.D.	do	do	do	11 7 6	John Smith his x mark	J.J.H.C.	49	35. 9/5
2 10 .	. . .		C.W.D.	do	do	do	8 10 6	E Foster	J.J.H.C.	50	57/5
. 1 .			C.W.D.	do	do	do	7 7 8	R. W. B. Freeman.	J.J.H.C.	51	55/5
5 10 .	. . .		C.W.D.	do	do	do	19 17 6	S. François	J.J.H.C.	52	46 46/5
										53	
										54	
										55	
										56	
										57	
										58	
										59	
										60	

29

* ...the Ship," thus "H.M.S. Revenge;" and the other Causes of leaving the Ship should be briefly stated thus, "Discharged," "Deserted," "Left Sick," "Died."

[Sixteen Pages.]

10 Name of

ACCOUNT OF APPRENTICES ON BOARD (IF ANY).

Christian and Surnames of the Apprentices at full length. 1	Year of Birth. 2	Registry of Indenture.		Date, Place, and Cause of leaving this Ship, or of Death. To be filled up by the Master.		
		Date of 3	Port of 4	Date. 5	Place. 6	Cause. 7
Robt. Wm. Beale Foreman	1862	1 July 79	London	Still by the ship		
Geo. Alex Fowler	1857	17 Aug 79	do			
Robt. Jas. Banyard	1864	21 Aug 80	do			
Thomas Lewis Thomas	1863	Sep 80	do			
Fredk. Walter Gifford	1865	2 July 81	do			
Frank Pratt Jameson	1864	5 July 81	do			
Baron V. C. Falck	1862	2 Sept 82	do	✗ Jan 4th 83	Sydney	Deserted

✗ The Master states that this desertion was omitted to be included in the endorsement. –

No Seaman [illegible]

No Stowaways [illegible]

CERTIFICATES

or Indorsements made by Consuls or by Officers in British Possessions Abroad.

Engaged (16)

I hereby certify that I have sanctioned the engagement of Isaac Francis C. Macintosh G. Francisco, W. Robertson, F. William Walter Grant, Andrew Golden, Emmanuel John Hall, Wm. George, Frank Bevan, Frank H. Fogh, [illegible] Rowland, Alick Nicholson, A. Smith, Wm. Smith upon the terms mentioned in the within written agreement, that I have ascertained and am satisfied that they fully understand the said agreement and have signed the same in my presence.

[signature]
Shipping Master
16/4/83

Discharged (12)

I certify that the within named F. Carter, Edwin Lewis, Wh. Le Babe, Walter Hill, Andrew Keely, F. Oliver, John Matthews, John Mitchell, B. O'Flaherty, Hy. Colman, J. Gordon, Albert Stevens, W. Cottam and James Lawrence have been discharged and left behind at this port on the alleged ground of mutual consent, that with the exception of (Le Babe) they all forfeited their wages up to their discharge and have removed their effects from the vessel.

[signature]
Shipping Master
16/4/83

Ship *Brilliant* 11

CERTIFICATES

or Indorsements made by Consuls or by Officers in British Possessions Abroad.

Deserted (5)

I hereby certify that the within named Chas Olsen John Randall J H Bowland Wm Smith and A Adcroft have been left behind at this Port on the alleged ground of having deserted that I have inquired into this matter and find the allegation true and that a proper entry of such desertion in the official log book has been produced to me.

[illegible]
Shipping Master

10/4/83

[Sixteen Pages.]

Ethiopian 1885 -1 886 Page 1

Eng. 1.

Executed in Sixteen Pages.

Any Erasure, Interlineation, or Alteration in this Agreement will be void unless attested by some Superintendent of a Mercantile Marine Office, Officer of Customs, Consul, or Vice-Consul, to be made with the consent of the persons interested.

RECEIVED. 21 JAN. 86

AGREEMENT AND ACCOUNT OF CREW.

FOREIGN-GOING SHIP.

The term "Foreign-going Ship" means every Ship employed in trading or going between some place or places in the United Kingdom and some place or places situate beyond the Coasts of the United Kingdom, the Islands of Guernsey, Jersey, Sark, Alderney, and Man, and the Continent of Europe between the River Elbe and Brest inclusive.

Issued by the Board of Trade, Nov., 1882. In pursuance of 17 & 18 Vict. c. 104.

Name of Ship.	Official No.	Port of Registry.	Port No. and Date of Register.	Registered Tonnage. Gross.	Net.	Nominal Horse power of Engines (if any).
Ethiopian	48859	Aberdeen	20 1864	838		

REGISTERED MANAGING OWNER.

Name.	Address. (State No. of House, Street, and Town.)	No. of Seamen for whom accommodation is certified. (30 & 31 Vict. c. 124.)	Distance in feet and inches between centre of the Disc showing the Maximum load line in salt water and upper edge of lines indicating the position of the Ship's decks above that centre. First Deck above it. ft.	in.	Second Deck above it. ft.	in.
Wm. Henderson	Aberdeen		4	3		

Scale of Provisions to be allowed and served out to the Crew during the Voyage, in addition to the daily issue of Lime and Lemon Juice and Sugar, or other antiscorbutics in any case required by 30th & 31st Vict., c. 124, s. 4.

	Bread	Beef	Pork	Flour	Peas	Rice	Tea	Coffee	Sugar	Water
Sunday	1	1½					⅛	½	2	3
Monday	1		1¼		½					
Tuesday	1	1½				⅓				
Wednesday	1		1¼		½					
Thursday	1	1½				⅓				
Friday	1		1¼		½					
Saturday	1	1½				⅓				

Note.—In any case an equal quantity of Fresh Meat or Fresh Vegetables may, at the option of the Master, be served out in lieu of the Salted or Tinned Meats or Preserved or Compressed Vegetables named in the above Scale.

SUBSTITUTES. NO SPIRITS ALLOWED

EQUIVALENT SUBSTITUTES AT THE MASTER'S OPTION

The several Persons whose names are hereto subscribed, and whose descriptions are contained on the other side or sides, and of whom 8 are engaged as Sailors, hereby agree to serve on board the said Ship, in the several capacities expressed against their respective Names, on a Voyage from[1]

London to Sydney and any Port or Places in Australia, New Zealand, India, China, Pacific, or Atlantic Oceans, West Indies, or America, trading backwards and forwards, as the Master may require, until the return of the vessel to a final Port of Discharge in the United Kingdom, calling at a Port for orders if required. Voyage not to exceed Two years.

And the Crew agree to conduct themselves in an orderly, faithful, honest, and sober manner, and to be at all times diligent in their respective duties, and to be obedient to the lawful commands of the said Master, or of any Person who shall lawfully succeed him, and of their Superior Officers, in everything relating to the said Ship and the Stores and Cargo thereof, whether on board, in boats, or on shore: in consideration of which Services to be duly performed, the said Master hereby agrees to pay to the said Crew as Wages the Sums against their Names respectively expressed, and to supply them with Provisions according to the above Scale. And it is hereby agreed, That any Embezzlement or wilful or negligent Destruction of any part of the Ship's Cargo or Stores shall be made good to the Owner out of the Wages of the Person guilty of the same: And if any Person enters himself as qualified for a duty which he proves incompetent to perform, his Wages shall be reduced in proportion to his incompetency: And it is also agreed, That the Regulations authorized by the Board of Trade, which are printed herein and numbered[2] 1. 2. 3 & 4.

are adopted by the parties hereto, and shall be considered as embodied in this Agreement: And it is also agreed, That if any Member of the Crew considers himself to be aggrieved by any breach of the Agreement or otherwise, he shall represent the same to the Master or Officer in charge of the Ship in a quiet and orderly manner, who shall thereupon take such steps as the case may require: And it is also agreed, That[3] Sixteen hands all told are to be considered the ship's full complement of Crew

In Witness whereof the said parties have subscribed their Names on the other Side or Sides hereof on the days against their respective Signatures mentioned.

Signed by Alex Jenkyns Master, on the 5th day of May 1885.

Date of Commencement of Voyage.	Port at which Voyage commenced.	Date of Termination of Voyage.	Port at which Voyage terminated.	Date of Delivery of Lists to Superintendent.	I hereby declare to the truth of the Entries in this Agreement and Account of Crew, &c.
5 May		6/1/86	London	7/1/86	Alex Jenkyns Master.

[1] Here the Voyage is to be described, and the places named at which the Ship is to touch, or, if that cannot be done, the general nature and probable length of the Voyage is to be stated.
[2] Here are to be inserted the numbers of any of the Regulations for preserving Discipline issued by the Board of Trade and printed on the last page hereof which the parties agree to adopt.
[3] Here any other stipulations may be inserted to which the parties agree, and which are not contrary to Law.

N.B.—This Form must not be unstitched. No leaves may be taken out of it, and none may be added or substituted. Care should be taken at the time of Engagement that a sufficiently large Form is used. If more men are engaged during the Voyage than the number for whom signatures are provided in this Form, an additional Form Eng. 1 should be obtained and used.

Sixteen pages.

Name of

PARTICULARS OF ENGAGEMENT.

Reference No.	Signatures of Crew.	Year of Birth.	Town or County where born.	If in the Reserve, No. of Commission or R.V.3.	Ship in which he last served, and Year of Discharge therefrom. Year.	State Name and Official No. or Port she belonged to.	Date and Place of signing this Agreement. Date.	Place.	In what Capacity engaged, and if Master, Mate, or Engineer, No. of Certificate.	Time at which he is to be on board.
1	2	3	4	5	6	7	8	9	10	
1	Alexr [illegible] (Master to sign first.)	1856	Aberdeen		1886	Same Ships	5.5.85	London	03158. Master	
2	Charles Cameron	1861	"		"	"	"	"	99782 Mate	6.5.85
3	W. J. Burge.	1860	Clifton		"	"	"	"	012572. 2nd Mate	
4	John Miller	1863.	Aberdeen		"	Kirkwood Lpool.	"	"	Carpr.	"
5	Alexr. Middleton	1862.	"		"	City of Aberdeen. Adeen	"	"	Stewd.	"
6	Joshua Scott	1851	Barbadoes		"	Dartmouth Ldon	6.5.85	"	Cook.	"
7	James Muckland?	1858	Aberdeen		"	Brilliant Adeen	5.5.85	"	Sails	"
8	James McDonald	1844.	"	75363?	"	Dunrobin Castle. "	"	"	Bosn	"
9	H W Pern.	1862	Hants		"	Norwegian Ship. Stavt?	"	"	AB	"
10	Andrew Aiken	1859	Aberdeen	74351.	"	Alex Nicol Adeen	"	"	AB	"
11	Andrew Andersen	1860	Norway		"	Pericles "	"	"	AB	"
12	Robt McKay	1861	Glasgow		"	Northern Empire Sunderl?	"	"	AB	"
13	John Archer	1840	Barbadoes		"	Same Ship	"	"	AB	"
14	Thomas Pennycott?	1859	Lpl		"	Marlboro. Gsgow.	"	"	AB	"
15	John Harris	1845.	Ldon		"	Dumbarton.	"	"	AB	"
16	Fredk Wipp?	1861.	Germany		"	Foreign Ships "	"	"	AB	"
17	John Glashan	1834.	Portsoy		"	Hawarden Castle Ldon	"	"	AB	"
18	A Baldwin.	1857	Jersey		"	Umgeni? Ldon.	"	"	AB	"
19	Frank Morice	1850	Montreal		"	Illawara. "	"	"	AB	"
20	Georg Woodcock	1865.	London		"	Miltiades Adeen	"	"	O.S.	"

* Engineers not employed on the Propelling Engines and Boilers

† If any Member of the Crew enters Her Majesty's Service, the Name of the Queen's Ship into which he enters is to be stated under the head of "Cause of leaving

8026 to 80299/5 3/7/85 77/1/3

Ship *Ethiopian*

Amount of Wages per ~~Week~~ or Calendar Month.	Advance agreed to.	Amount of ~~Weekly~~ or Monthly Allotment.	Signature or Initials of Superintendent, Consul, or Officer of Customs.	PARTICULARS OF DISCHARGE, &c. Date	Place	Cause.†	Balance of Wages paid on Discharge.	RELEASE (note M). We, the undersigned Members of the Crew of this Ship, do hereby release this Ship and the Master and Owner or Owners thereof, from all Claims for Wages, or otherwise in respect of this Voyage. Signatures of Crew (each to be on the Line on which he signed in Col. 1).	Signatures or Initials of Official before whom the Balance of Wages was paid and Release signed.	Reference No.	
11	12	13	14	15	16	17	18	19	20		
...	...	...	Immosed	Remains						1	
7 10		3 15 . 2		7/9/85	Sydney	Dis	11 13 9	Cameron			
5		2 10 . 2		7/1/86	London	Dis	14 6 0	W. J. Burge	WL	3	68/9
5	2 10	2 10		do	do	do	5 15 0	J. Miller	WL	4	75/5
4	2	2		do	do	do	3 4 9	A. Middleton	WL	5	
4 5		2 2 6 2		do	do	do	2 3 5	J Scott	WL	6	70 to 75
4	2	2		do	do	do	7 9 9	J. Macklane	WL	7	74
4		2 . 2		do	do	do	18 15 8	James F. McDonald ~~[illegible]~~	WL	8	
1	To be disch.d at Sydney			13/8/85	Sydney	Dis	1 7 6	H W Dern			
2 15		1 7 6 2		7/1/86	London	Dis	8 14 6	A Aiken	WL	10	84
2 15		1 7 6 2		5/10/85	Sydney	Deserted	~~See Log Page 15 as to his name being omitted from endorsement~~			11	a.s
2 15		1 7 6 2		7/1/86	London	Dis	8 18 0	R. McNay	WL	12	83
2 15		1 7 6 2		do	do	do	14 12	John Arch	WL	13	78
2 15		1 7 6 2		31/8/85	Sydney	Deserted			a.s	14	
2 15		1 7 6 2		7/1/86	London	Dis	13 18	Jn Harris	WL	15	79/80
2 15		1 7 6 2		31/8/85	Sydney	Deserted			a.s	16	
2 15		1 7 6 2		do	do	do			a.s	17	
2 15		1 7 6 2		26/8/85	Sydney	Dis	Nil	A Baldwin		18	
2 15		1 7 6 2		31/8/85	do	Deserted			a.s	19	
1 10		15 . 2		2/10/85	do	do			a.s	20	

Note The figures on the right of the allotment column denote the number of payments for which the Note is drawn. Those without similar figures are for payment during the Voyage

... should be described as Engine Drivers here and in Dis. 1.
... the Ship," thus, "H.M.S. Revenge;" and the other Causes of leaving the Ship should be briefly stated thus, "Discharged," "Deserted," "Left Sick," "Died."

Ethiopian 1885 - 1886 Page 4

4 *Name of*

PARTICULARS OF ENGAGEMENT.

Reference No.	SIGNATURES OF CREW.	Year of Birth.	Town or County where born.	If in the Reserve, No. of Commission or R V 2.	Ship in which he last served, and Year of Discharge therefrom. Year.	State Name and Official No. or Port she belonged to.	Date and place of signing this Agreement. Date.	Place.	In what Capacity engaged, and if Master, Mate, or Engineer, No. of Certificate.*	Time at which he is to be on board.
	1	2	3	4	5	6	7	8	9	10
21	William Nelson	25	L'pool			Shore Service	29/9/85	Sydney	AB	[illegible]
22	George H. Wiseman?	38	Kent			[illegible]	29/9/85	Do	AB	Do
23	W. G. Colbeck	18	[illegible]			Derwent	29/9/85	Do	Boy	Do
24	G. M. Hardy	54	Aberdeen			[illegible]	29/9/85	Do	1553? 2nd Mate	25/9/85
25	James Cumming	37	Shields			[illegible]	29/9/85	Do	AB	1/10/85
26	W. Payne	38	London			[illegible]	29/9/85	Do	AB	Do
27	Frederick Gibbons	22	Do			[illegible]	30/9/85	Do	AB	Do
28	Jno. E. Brooks	25	Canada			This Ship	30/9/85	Do	[illegible]	Do
29	Wm Leggatt	26	Lanark			Shore Service	30/9/85	Do	Do	Do
30										
31										
32										
33										
34										
35										
36										
37										
38										
39										
40										

* Engineers not employed on the Propelling Engines and Boilers

† If any Member of the Crew enters Her Majesty's Service, the Name of the Queen's Ship into which he enters is to be stated under the head of "*Cause of leaving*

Ship Ethiopian

Amount of Wages per Week, or Calendar Month. (11)	Advance agreed to. (12)	Amount of Weekly or Monthly Allotment. (13)	Signature or Initials of Superintendent, Consul, or Officer of Customs. (14)	PARTICULARS OF DISCHARGE, &c., To be filled in by the Master upon the Discharge, Death or Desertion of any Member of his Crew. Date, Place, and Cause of leaving this Ship, or of Death. Date. (15)	Place. (16)	Cause.† (17)	Balance of Wages paid on Discharge. (18)	RELEASE (late M). We, the undersigned Members of the Crew of this Ship, do hereby release this Ship and the Master and Owner or Owners thereof, from all Claims for Wages, or otherwise in respect of this Voyage. Signatures of Crew (each to be on the Line on which he signed in Col. 1). (19)	Signature or Initials of Official before whom the Balance of Wages was paid and Release signed. (20)	Reference No.
5 . .	5 . .		James Murphy	6/1/86	London	Dis.		William Robson	W Lane Supt. Mer. Mar. Office.	21
5 . .	3 10 .		[illegible]	do	do	do	11 9 8	George H. F. Hodgman	WL	89/90
4 . .			[illegible]	do	do	do	=	W. G. Colbeck	WL	23
8 . .			[illegible]	do	do	do	4 19 0	J. McHardy		24
5 . .	5 . .		[illegible]	do	do	do		James Cunningham	W Lane Supt. Mer. Mar. Office.	25
5 . .	5 . .		[illegible]	do	do	do	8 15 6	[illegible]	WL	26 88
5 . .	2 10 .	pd.	[illegible]	do	do	do	12 6 8	[illegible]	WL	27 81/2
4 . .			[illegible]	do	do	do	=	Geo. C. Brooks	WL	28
1 1 .			[illegible]	do	do	do	=	Wm Leggatt	WL	29
										30
										31
				19						32
										33
										34
										35
										36
										37
										38
										39
										40

should be described as Engine Drivers here and in Dis. 1.
the Ship," thus, "H.M.S. Revenge," and the other Causes of leaving the Ship should be briefly stated thus, "Discharged," "Deserted," "Left Sick," "Died."

Sixteen pages.

10 *Name of*

ACCOUNT OF APPRENTICES ON BOARD (IF ANY).

Christian and Surname of the Apprentices at full length. 1.	Year of Birth. 2.	Registry of Indenture. Date of 3.	Port of 4.	Date, Place, and Cause of leaving this Ship, or of Death. To be filled up by the Master. Date. 5.	Place. 6.	Cause. 7.
Alfred Hottley	1866	7.5.83	London	Still	by	the Ship
Walter Wightman	1867	12.5.84	"	do	—	do
Hy R. C. Fletcher	1869	1.5.85	"	do	—	do
G. F. S. Allen	1869	4.5.85	"	do	—	do

No Scurvy WL   No Stowaways WL

CERTIFICATES

Or Indorsements made by Consuls or by Officers in British Possessions Abroad.

Engaged (9)

The within written seamen vizt. Wm Nelson Geo Hodgman W E Colbeck E H Hardy Jas Cunningham Thos Payne J Gibbons Robt Brooks & Wm Leggatt have been engaged at this port upon the terms of the within written agreement which they have signed in my presence

Discharged (3)

The following seamen vizt C Cameron J W Penn and A Baldwin have been discharged at this port on the ground of mutual consent and that the two former seamen received the wages set against their names

Deserted (5)

The following seamen vizt Frank Morice Fred Weske J Gallagher Thos Penny and George Woodcock have been left at this port as deserters and that a proper entry of such desertions in the Official log has been produced to me.

2/10/85

H. Brown
Shipping Master

1887

Eng. 1.

Executed in Sixteen Pages.

Any Erasure, Interlineation, or Alteration in this Agreement will be void unless attested by some Superintendent of a Mercantile Marine Office, Officer of Customs, Consul, or Vice-Consul, to be made with the consent of the persons interested.

AGREEMENT AND ACCOUNT OF CREW.

FOREIGN-GOING SHIP.

The term "Foreign-going Ship" means every Ship employed in trading or going between some place or places in the United Kingdom and some place or places situate beyond the Coasts of the United Kingdom, the Islands of Guernsey, Jersey, Sark, Alderney, and Man, and the Continent of Europe between the River Elbe and Brest inclusive.

Issued by the Board of Trade, Nov., 1882, in pursuance of 17 & 18 Vict. c. 104. 22/7 26.7

Name of Ship.	Official No.	Port of Registry.	Port No. and Date of Register.	Registered Tonnage. Gross.	Net.	Nominal Horse-power of Engines (if any).
Ballochmyle	67930	Dundee	11 / 1883	1510	1438	—

Registered Managing Owner. Name.	Address. (State No. of House, Street and Town.)	No. of Seamen for whom accommodation is certified. (30 & 31 Vict. c. 124.)	Distance in feet and inches between centre of the Disc showing the Maximum load line in salt water and upper edge of lines indicating the position of the Ship's decks above that centre. First Deck above it. ft. in.	Second Deck above it. ft. in.
David Bruce & Co	Royal Exchange Place Dundee	48	4 – 2	—

Scale of Provisions to be allowed and served out to the Crew during the Voyage, in addition to the daily issue of Lime and Lemon Juice and Sugar, or other antiscorbutics in any case required by 30th & 31st Vict., c. 124, s. 4.

Sunday	1	1½					½		⅛	½	2	3		
Monday	1		1¼					⅓						
Tuesday	1	1½					½							
Wednesday	1		1¼					⅓	Daily					
Thursday	1	1½					½							
Friday	1		1¼					⅓						
Saturday	1	1½					½							

Note.—In any case an equal quantity of Fresh Meat or Fresh Vegetables may, at the option of the Master, be served out in lieu of the Salted or Tinned Meats or Preserved or Compressed Vegetables named in the above Scale.

SUBSTITUTES.

Equivalent Substitutes as may be found necessary.

The several Persons whose names are hereto subscribed, and whose descriptions are contained on the other side or sides, and of whom ______ are engaged as Sailors, hereby agree to serve on board the said Ship, in the several capacities expressed against their respective Names, on a Voyage from[1] the Tay to Frederickstadt, thence to Melbourne, and or any ports or places not exceeding 75° North and 65° South Latitudes trading within these limits as required, for a period not exceeding Three Years, and back to a final port of discharge in the United Kingdom, or on the Continent of Europe, between the Elbe and Brest, with power to call at any place for orders.

And it is agreed that the position of the ... line ... which ... indicates the freeboard shall not be altered so long as this present agreement is in force, and it is further agreed that if during the Winter months this vessel is at any time engaged in the North Atlantic trade she shall be so loaded that the centre of the disc shall not be less than (in.) inches out of water in salt water. [handwritten across: "not required" / W Howdon Master]

And the Crew agree to conduct themselves in an orderly, faithful, honest, and sober manner, and to be at all times diligent in their respective duties, and to be obedient to the lawful commands of the said Master, or of any Person who shall lawfully succeed him, and of their Superior Officers, in everything relating to the said Ship and the Stores and Cargo thereof, whether on board, in boats, or on shore: in consideration of which Services to be duly performed, the said Master hereby agrees to pay to the said Crew as Wages the Sums against their Names respectively expressed, and to supply them with Provisions according to the above Scale. And it is hereby agreed, That any Embezzlement or wilful or negligent Destruction of any part of the Ship's Cargo or Stores shall be made good to the Owner out of the Wages of the Person guilty of the same: And if any Person enters himself as qualified for a duty which he proves incompetent to perform, his Wages shall be reduced in proportion to his incompetency: And it is also agreed, That the Regulations authorized by the Board of Trade, which are printed herein and numbered[2] 1 to 4 inclusive are adopted by the parties hereto, and shall be considered as embodied in this Agreement: And it is also agreed, That if any Member of the Crew considers himself to be aggrieved by any breach of the Agreement or otherwise, he shall represent the same to the Master or Officer in charge of the Ship in a quiet and orderly manner, who shall thereupon take such steps as the case may require: And it is also agreed, That[3] all monies advanced and wages paid in India shall be charged at the exchange of Two Shillings per Rupee, and in America at Four Shillings and Sixpence per Dollar, Also that five per cent commission shall be charged on all monies advanced in the Colonies, And further, should any of the crew demand and obtain his discharge in the Colonies, his wages shall be paid at the rate of One Shilling per Month in lieu of the wages within specified, and further, that the Ship shall be deemed fully manned with Twenty-four hands all told.

In Witness whereof the said parties have subscribed their Names on the other Side or Sides hereof on the days against their respective Signatures mentioned.

Signed by W Howdon Master, on the 7th day of April 1886.

Date of Commencement of Voyage.	Port at which Voyage commenced.	Date of Termination of Voyage.	Port at which Voyage terminated.	Date of Delivery of Lists to Superintendent.	I hereby declare to the truth of the Entries in this Agreement and Account of Crew, &c.
7/4/86	Dundee	10 July/87	Liverpool	11/7/87	W Howdon Master.

(Last four columns: These Columns to be filled up at the end of the Voyage.)

[1] Here the Voyage is to be described, and the places named at which the Ship is to touch, or, if that cannot be done, the general nature and probable length of the Voyage is to be stated.
[2] Here are to be inserted the numbers of any of the Regulations for preserving Discipline issued by the Board of Trade and printed on the last page hereof which the parties agree to adopt.
[3] Here any other stipulations may be inserted to which the parties agree, and which are not contrary to Law.

N.B.—This Form must not be unstitched. No leaves may be taken out of it, and none may be added or substituted. Care should be taken at the time of Engagement that a sufficiently large Form is used. If more men are engaged during the Voyage than the number for whom signatures are provided in this Form, additional Form Eng. 1 should be obtained and used.

J. & M. 800 9/84

Ballochmyle 1886 - 1887 Page 2

 Name of

PARTICULARS OF ENGAGEMENT.

Reference No.	Signatures of Crew.	Year of Birth	Town or County where born.	If in the Reserve, No. of Commission or R.V.2.	Ship in which he last served, and Year of Discharge therefrom: Year	State Name and Official No. or Port she belonged to.	Date and Place of signing this Agreement: Date	Place	In what Capacity engaged, and if Master, Mate, or Engineer, No. of Certificate.*	Time at which he is to be on board.
1	W. Bowden (Master to sign first)	57.	Ipswich			Ballochmyle (Dundee)	Continued		10260	
2	[illegible]	25	Falkirk		1886	do	7.4.86	Dundee	Mate 09595	10th April 6 a.m.
3	Thos Cammond	21	Forfarshire		"	Routenburn (Greenock)	do		2nd Mate 015315	do
4	Francis Dick	33	Aberdeen	71520	"	Othello (Liverpool)	do	do	Steward	do
5	William Carter	46	~~Kingston~~ (Jamaica)		"	Medusa (London)	do	do	Cook	do
6	James Robertson	28	Aberdeen		"	Kelvinside (Glasgow)	do	do	Carptr	do
7	James Macfland	27	"		"	Ethiopia (Aberdeen)	8.4.86	do	Sailmaker	do
8	~~William Jones~~		~~Newcastle~~		"	Ballochmyle (Dundee)	do	do	~~Boy~~	do
9	Patrick Haskins	27 ~~35~~	Boston		"	Santiago	9.4.86	GLASGOW	AB	8.30 a.m. Buchanan 10.4.86
10	John Farquhar	25	Wick		1885	Star of Scotia (Bfast)	"	"	AB	"
11	G. Harms	38	Germany		1886	Mulgrave	"	"	AB	"
12	Paul [illegible]	24	Glasgow		"	Syren (Gk)	"	"	~~AB~~	"
13	Ingeval Larson	25	Norway		"	Lady Isabella (Gw)	"	"	AB	"
14	[illegible]	39	Copenhagen		"	Stracathro (Gk)	"	"	~~AB~~	"
15	x Edward Lake	40	Halifax		"	do	"	"	AB	"
16	Chas. Carls	30	Queenstown		1885	Yuca (Lpl)	"	"	~~AB~~	"
17	Samuel Hounsell	19	Greenock		1886	Natalla (Gw)	"	"	AB	"
18	Thomas Bannatyne	21	Arran		"	John Banfield	"	"	AB	"
19	~~W. Watson~~	30	~~Finland~~		"	Aristides (Adn)	"	"	~~AB~~	"
20	James Cunningham	50	G'gow		"	Devonia (Bw)	"	"	AB	"

* Engineers not employed on the Propelling Engines and Boilers

† If any Member of the Crew enters Her Majesty's Service, the Name of the Queen's Ship into which he enters is to be stated under the head of "Cause of leaving"

Ship *Ballochmyle* **3**

first Amount of Wages per Calendar Month. (11)	Amount of Wages each Subsequent Month (12)	Amount of Monthly Allotment. (13)	Signature or Initials of Superintendent, Consul, or Officer of Customs. (14)	PARTICULARS OF DISCHARGE, &c., To be filled in by the Master upon the Discharge, Death or Desertion of any Member of his Crew. Date, Place, and Cause of leaving this Ship, or of Death. Date. (15)	Place. (16)	Cause. (17)	Balance of Wages paid on Discharge. (18)	RELEASE (see M). We, the undersigned Members of the Crew of this Ship, do hereby release this Ship and the Master and Owner or Owners thereof, from all Claims for Wages, or otherwise in respect of this Voyage. Signatures of Crew (each to be on the Line on which he signed in Col. 1). (19)	Signature or Initials of Official before whom the Balance of Wages was paid and Release signed. (20)	Release No.
			[illegible]	Remains						1
1 . .	8 . .	4 . .	M	10/7/87	Lpool	dischg	£ 40 14 4	[illegible]	[illegible]	2
5 . .	5 . .	2 10 .	M	do	do	do	18 19 9	Thos C [illegible]	WR	3
2 10 .	5 . .	2 10 .	M	do	do	do	24 8 9	Francis Dick	WR	4
1 . .	4 . .	. .	M	25/5/86	[illegible]	Dischgd	2 1 .	William Carter	[illegible]	5
6 . .	6 . .	3 . .	M	10/7/87	Lpool	dischg	40 11 5	Wages received on behalf of James Robertson	WR	6
2 5 .	4 10 .	2 5 .	[illegible]	do	do	do	26 14 5	Wages received on behalf of James Macklaine	WR	7
1 15 .	3 10 .	2 . .	[illegible]	20/11/86	[illegible]	[illegible]		(official log page 16)		8
per month 2 15	first month after		[illegible]	Did not join				[illegible]		9
1/- 2 15	first month after		K	10/7/87	Lpool	Dischg	29 6 9	Wages received on behalf of John Farquhar	WR	10
1/- 2 15	first month after		K	do	do	do	28 8 10	G. Harons	WR	11
1/- 2 15	first month after		K	30/9/86	[illegible]	[illegible]		[illegible]	[illegible]	12
1/- 2 15	first month after		K	10/7/87	Lpool	dischg	17 1 9	Ingvard Larsen	WR	13
1/- 2 15	first month after		K	Did not join				[illegible]		14
1/- 2 15	first month after		K	10/7/87	Lpool	dischg	31 13 4	Wages received on behalf of Edward Lake	WR	15
1/- 2 15	first month after		K	30/9/86	[illegible]	[illegible]		Chas his x mark Carl	[illegible]	16
1/- 2 15	first month after		K	10/7/87	Lpool	dischg	19 14 0	S. Hounsell	WR	17
1/- 2 15	first month after		K	do	do	do	25 8 10	Wages received on behalf of Thomas Baundyple	WR	18
1/- 2 15	first month after		K	Did not join				[illegible]		19
1/- 2 15	first month after		K	10/7/87	Lpool	dischg	30 13 1	[illegible]	WR	20

should be described as Engine Drivers here and in Dis. 1.
the Ship," thus, "H.M.S. Revenge;" and the other Causes of leaving the Ship should be briefly stated thus, "Discharged," "Deserted," "Left Sick," "Died."

Sixteen pages.

Ballochmyle 1886 - 1887 Page 4

4 — *Name of*

PARTICULARS OF ENGAGEMENT.

Reference No.	Signatures of Crew.	Year of Birth.	Town or County where born.	If in the Reserve, No. of Commission or R V 2.	Ship in which he last served, and Year of Discharge therefrom. Year.	State Name and Official No. or Port she belonged to.	Date and place of signing this Agreement. Date.	Place.	In what Capacity engaged, and if Master, Mate, or Engineer, No. of Certificate.*	Time at which he is to be on board.
1	1	2	3	4	5	6	7	8	9	10
21	Charles Bernholdt	22	Hamburg		1886	Diamond	9.4.86	GLASGOW	AB	8.30 am Buchanan St. 10.4.86
22	Alexander Hutchison	23	Dundee		"	Ballochmyle	7.4.86	Dundee	OS	10.4.86 6 am
23	Peter X Falconer	22	do		"	do	do	do	OS	do
24	William Andrews	19	do		"	do	do	do	OS	do
25	Anton Danielson	25	Sweden		"	Marion Crosby Glasgow	10.4.86	do	AB	at once
26	Anton Pedersen	31	Norway		"	Foreign Ship	24/5 86	Frederikstad [illegible]	[illegible]	26/5
27	Gustav Jönsson	30	Sweden		84	do	do	do	AB	26/5
28	Carl Andersen	24	Norway		86	do	do	do	AB	26/5
29	Ole Theodor Larsen	43	do		do	do	25/5 86	do	AB	26/5
30	Robert Harris	49	Barbados		Port	[illegible]	23/10/86		Cook	23/10/86
31	John Bramfield	[illegible]	[illegible]		1886	Bonanza	29/10/86	Melbourne	AB	2/11/86
32	W[illegible]	25	[illegible]		do	do	do		AB	do
33	[illegible]	32	[illegible]		do	Scottish [illegible]	do		AB	do
34	[illegible] Stewart	24	America		do	[illegible]	do		AB	do
35	Henry Lynch	22	[illegible]		Port	[illegible]	do		AB	29/10/86
36	Wm Christ	26	[illegible]		do	[illegible]	[illegible]/10/86		AB	2/11/86
37	Edmund Sandlin	26	Philadelphia		do	American Ship	6/11/86	[illegible]	AB	6/11/86
38	William Johnson his X mark	38	Jamaica			do	6/11/86	do	AB	6/11/86
39	Joseph Dyke	33	North Wales			Gilarmo	25/2/87	Astoria	AB.	26/2/87 [illegible]
40	O. C. Moore	35	N Carolina			Ville Hermine	do	do	do	26/2/87

* Engineers not employed on the Propelling Engines and Boilers

† If any Member of the Crew enters Her Majesty's Service, the Name of the Queen's Ship into which he enters is to be stated under the head of "Cause of leaving"

Ballochmyle 1886 - 1887 Page 5

Ship *Ballochmyle* **5**

Amount of Wages per Week, or Calendar Month.	Advance agreed to.	Amount of Weekly or Monthly Allotment.	Signature or Initials of Superintendent, Consul, or Officer of Customs.	PARTICULARS OF DISCHARGE, &c., To be filled in by the Master upon the Discharge, Death or Desertion of any Member of his Crew. Date, Place, and Cause of leaving this Ship, or of Death — Date.	Place.	Cause.†	Balance of Wages paid on Discharge.	RELEASE (date M). We, the undersigned Members of the Crew of this Ship, do hereby release this Ship and the Master and Owner or Owners thereof, from all Claims for Wages, or otherwise in respect of this Voyage. Signatures of Crew (each to be on the Line on which he signed in Col. 1).	Signature or Initials of Official before whom the Balance of Wages was paid and Release signed.	Reference No.
11	12	13	14	15	16	17	18	19	20	
1/- 2 15	first month after		[illegible]	10/7/87	Lpool	dischgd	27 7 1	Charles Bornholdt	WN	21
1 . (Amount of wages for first Calendar month)	2 5 . (Amount of advance & allotment)	.	A. [illegible]	28 Jan/87	Portland	Deserted	See	Off log book pg 18	R	22
. 1	2 5 .	.	"	~~14/7/87~~	~~Lpool~~ Didn't join	~~dischgd~~				23
. 1 .	1 10 .	.	"	30/9/86 do	Melbourne do	deserted do				24
1/- 2 15	first month after		G. Begg Dy	30/9/86	Melbourne	deserted	(See Official Log page 16)			25
2 15 .	2 15	X	E. T.	30/9/88	Mellbn	dis	mc	J. Pedersen	mn	26
2 10	2 10	X	E. T.	do	do	do	mc	~~H Johansson~~ E. Jönson	mn	27
2 10	2 10	X	E. T.	30/9/86	Melbourne	deserted	(See Official Log page 16)			28
2 10	2 10	X	E. T.	30/9/88	Mellbn	dis	Mc	T. Johansen	mn	29
4 —		X	R Whi[illegible]	10/7/87	Lpool	dischgd	30 9 11	Wages received on behalf of Robert Harres under sec. 4 (b) of Act 43 & 44 Vict. chap. 16.	WN Supt. Mer. Office	30
3 10	[illegible]	X	mn	28 Jan/87	Portland	Deserted	See	official log book p 18	R	31
3 10	3 10	X	mn	do	do	do		do	R.	32
3 10	3 10	X	mn	10/7/87	Lpool	dischgd	22 17 6	James Kenrick	WN	33
3 10	3 15	X	mn	do	do	do	9 7 0	James Stewart	WN	34
3 10		X	mn	28 Jan/87	Portland	Deserted	See	official log book p 18	R	35
3 10	3 15	X	mn	Did not join						36
3 10	3 - -	V	Pilot Samuel Edwards	10/7/87	Lpool	dischgd	9 9 2	Edmund [illegible]	WN	37
3 10	3 10 0	V	Pilot Samuel Edwards	28 Jan/87	Portland	Deserted	See	official log book p 18	R.	38
5 0 0		one of £8 0 0	P. L. C	10/7/87	Lpool	dischgd	13 1 0	Joseph Dyke	WN	39
5 0 0		one of £8 0 0	P. L. C	do	do	do	13 13 0	Ole Olsen	WN	40

...should be described as Engine Drivers here and in Dis. 1.
...the Ship," thus, "H.M.S. Revenge," and the other Causes of leaving the Ship should be briefly stated thus, "Discharged," "Deserted," "Left Sick," "Died."

Sixteen pages

Ballochmyle 1886 - 1887 Page 6

Name of

PARTICULARS OF ENGAGEMENT.

Reference No.	SIGNATURES OF CREW.	Year of Birth.	Town or County where born.	If in the Reserve, No. of Commission or R.V.I.	Ship in which he last served, and Year of Discharge therefrom. Year.	State Name and Official No. or Port she belonged to.	Date and place of signing this Agreement. Date.	Place.	In what Capacity engaged, and if Master, Mate, or Engineer, No. of Certificate.*	Time at which he is to be on board.
	1	2	3	4	5	6	7	8	9	10
41	C. Dann	23	Northampton		86	J B Brown	25/2/87	Astoria	O.S.	26/2/87
42	Wilhelm Menken	23	Germany		87	Snow & Burgess	do	do	AB	do
43	J Mattson	31	Gothenburg		87	do	do	do	do	do
44	~~J Mattson~~									
45										
46	W. F. Kinsey ✓	19	London		1/68	Same Ship	10th May 1887	At Sea	AB	Same
47										
48										
49										
50										
51										
52										
53										
54										
55										
56										
57										
58										
59										
60										

* Engineers not employed on the Propelling Engines and Boilers

† If any Member of the Crew enters Her Majesty's Service, the Name of the Queen's Ship into which he enters is to be stated under the head of "Cause of leaving"

Ballochmyle 1886 - 1887 Page 7

Ship ____________

Amount of Wages per Week, or Calendar Month.	Advance agreed to.	Amount of Weekly or Monthly Allotment.	Signature or Initials of Superintendent, Consul, or Officer of Customs.	PARTICULARS OF DISCHARGE, &c., To be filled in by the Master upon the Discharge, Death or Desertion of any Member of his Crew. Date, Place, and Cause of leaving this Ship, or of Death. Date.	Place.	Cause.†	Balance of Wages paid on Discharge.	RELEASE (late M). We, the undersigned Members of the Crew of this Ship, do hereby release this Ship and the Master and Owner or Owners thereof, from all Claims for Wages, or otherwise in respect of this Voyage. Signatures of Crew (each to be on the Line on which he signed in Col. 1).	Signature or Initials of Official before whom the Balance of Wages was paid and Release signed.	Reference No.
11	12	13	14	15	16	17	18	19	20	
3 0 0	/	one of £8 0 0	V.L.C	10/7/87	Lpool	dischgd	4 10 0	C. Dann	WR	41
5 0 0	/	one of £8 0 0	V.L.C	do	do	do	13 1 2	J. Mason	WR	42
5 0 0	/	one of £8 0 0	V.L.C	do	do	do	14 7 6	T. Munro	WR	43
										44
~~2 10 0~~										45
2 15 0	✓	✓	Sees. ✓ O. Hoye 21.	do	do	do	Nil	A. Kinsey	WR	46
										47
										48
										49
										50
										51
										52
										53
										54
										55
										56
										57
										58
										59
										60

should be described as Engine Drivers here and in Dis. 1.
the Ship," thus, "H.M.S. Revenge;" and the other Causes of leaving the Ship should be briefly stated thus, "Discharged," "Deserted," "Left Sick," "Died."

Sixteen pages.

ACCOUNT OF APPRENTICES ON BOARD (IF ANY).

Christian and Surnames of the Apprentices at full length. 1.	Age 2.	Registry of Indenture.		Date, Place, and Cause of leaving this Ship, or of Death. To be filled up by the Master.		
		Date of 3	Port of 4	Date. 5.	Place. 6.	Cause. 7.
Albert Frederick Kinsey	17	11.5.83	London	18.5.87	At Sea	Time Expired Sec. No. 46
William Graham Lawson	18	29.3.86	Dundee	10/7/87	Lpool	Remains
Alfred Brewer Adams	18	8.4.86	London	15th May 1886	Fredrikstadt	Mutual Consent
Walter Cave	19	10.4.86	do	10/7/87	Lpool	Remains

CERTIFICATES

Or Indorsements made by Consuls or by Officers in British Possessions Abroad.

I certify that the above named Alfred Brewer Adams has been written off the articles by mutual consent.

Fredrikstad 15 May 1886
Carsten Thiis
British Viceconsul

BRITISH VICE-CONSULATE FREDERIKSSTADT

British Vice Consulate
Fredrikstad

I hereby certify, that the within named William Carter has been discharged and left behind at this port, on the alleged ground of mutual consent, that I have inquired into the matter and find that the allegation is true, and that I have accordingly granted my sanction to his being so left, and that £2-1-. being wages due to him up to 25 May have been duly paid to me in cash.

I also certify, that I have sanctioned the engagement of Anton Pedersen, Gustav Jönsson, Carl Andersen, Ole Theodor Johansen upon the terms mentioned in the within written agreement that I have am satisfied, that

Ballochmyle 1886 - 1887 Page 9

Ship "Ballochmyle" 11

CERTIFICATES

Or Indorsements made by Consuls or by Officers in British Possessions Abroad.

that they fully understand the said agreement, and that they have signed the same in my presence.

Articles deposited 16 April 1886.
returned 25 May "

BRITISH VICE-CONSULATE FREDERIKSSTADT

Edward Thrst [signature]

Acting British Vice Consul

15812 2s.
TWO SHILLINGS
BRITISH VICE-CONSULATE FREDERIKSSTADT

Melbourne Nov 1st 1886

Vessel arrived 23/9/86
Articles deposited 24/9/86

do returned today

I hereby certify that the within-named J Snadden Chas Carr J Petersen J Johanson & G Jonsson have been discharged at this port on the ground of mutual consent, and that they have signed their "Release" without wages before me; also that the within named A Danielson Carl Anderson & H Jones have been left behind at this port on the alleged ground of their having deserted, and that the proper entries of such desertions in the Official Log Book have been produced to me; I also certify that I have sanctioned the engagement of Robt Harris Jas Bransfield Wm Gemmel Chas Lamott Jas Stewart Ed Lynch and William Christ upon the terms mentioned in the within-written agreement, that I am satisfied they fully understand the said agreement, and have signed the same in my presence.

J. A. Rowway [signature]
SUPERINTENDENT
MERCANTILE MARINE OFFICE

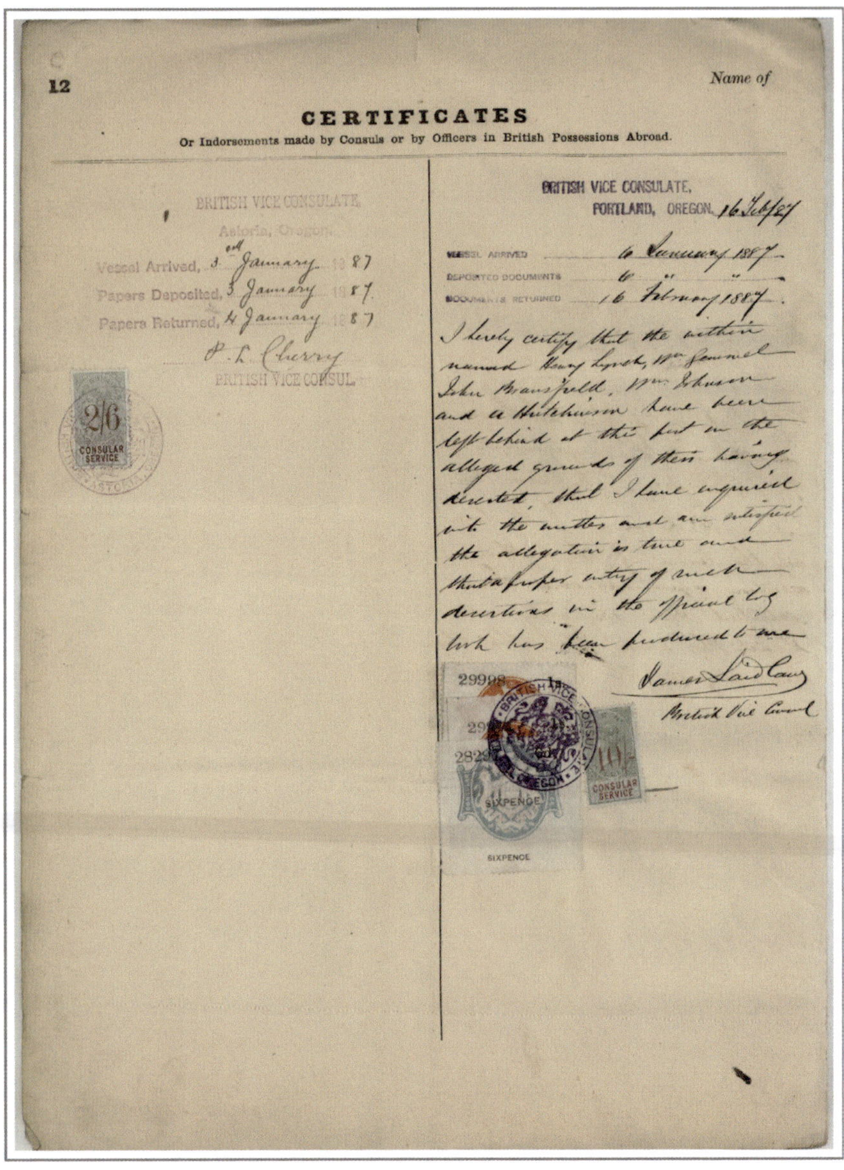

12

Name of

CERTIFICATES

Or Indorsements made by Consuls or by Officers in British Possessions Abroad.

BRITISH VICE CONSULATE,
Astoria, Oregon.

Vessel Arrived, 3rd January 1887
Papers Deposited, 3 January 1887
Papers Returned, 4 January 1887

P. L. Cherry
BRITISH VICE CONSUL.

2/6 CONSULAR SERVICE

BRITISH VICE CONSULATE,
PORTLAND, OREGON. 16 Feb/87

VESSEL ARRIVED 6 January 1887.
DEPOSITED DOCUMENTS 6 " "
DOCUMENTS RETURNED 16 February 1887.

I hereby certify that the within named Henry Lynch, Wm Sommel, John Mansfield, Wm Johnson and A Hutchinson have been left behind at this port on the alleged grounds of their having deserted, that I have enquired into the matter and am satisfied the allegation is true and that a proper entry of such desertions in the official log book has been produced to me

James Laidlaw
British Vice Consul

BRITISH VICE CONSULATE PORTLAND OREGON

10/- CONSULAR SERVICE

SIXPENCE

Ballochmyle 1886 - 1887 Page 11

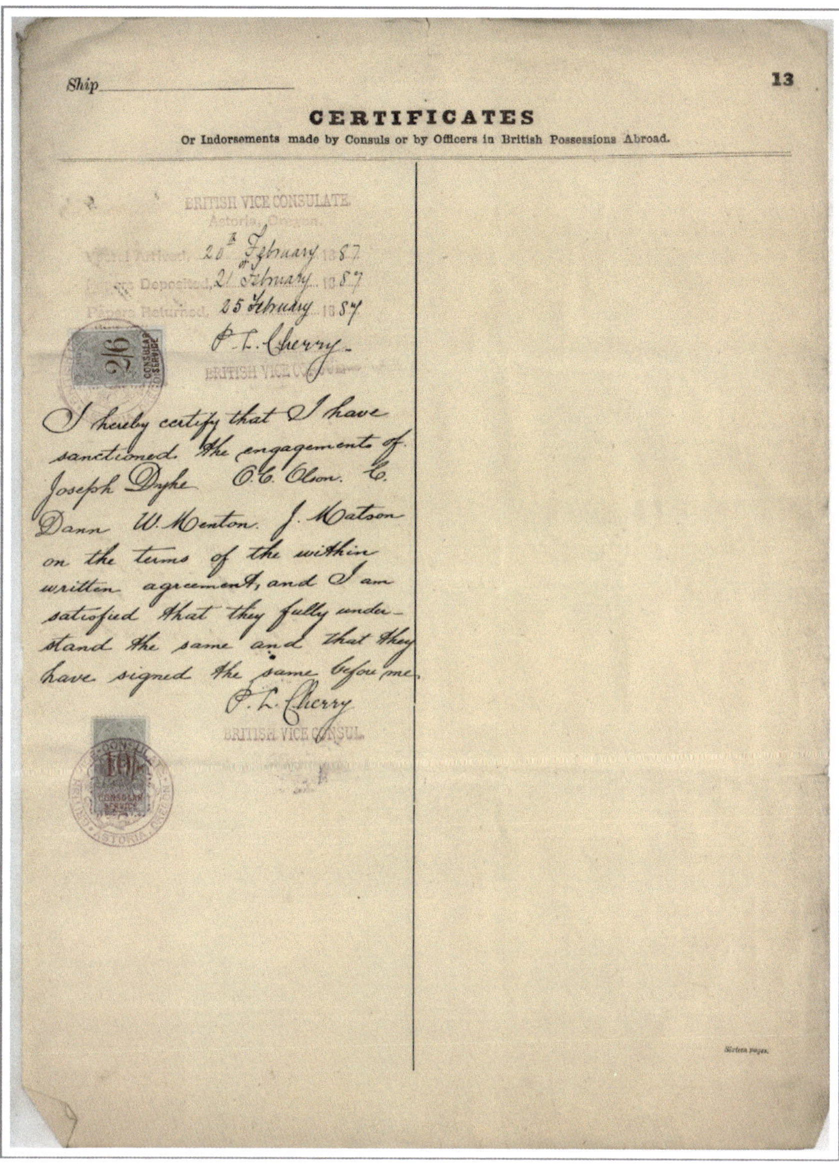
Ship ______________ 13

CERTIFICATES

Or Indorsements made by Consuls or by Officers in British Possessions Abroad.

BRITISH VICE CONSULATE.
Astoria, Oregon.

Vessel Arrived, 20th February 1887
Papers Deposited, 21st February 1887
Papers Returned, 25 February 1887

P. L. Cherry
BRITISH VICE CONSUL

2/6 CONSULAR SERVICE

I hereby certify that I have sanctioned the engagement of Joseph Dyke C.C. Olson C. Dann W. Menton J. Matson on the terms of the within written agreement, and I am satisfied that they fully understand the same and that they have signed the same before me.

P. L. Cherry
BRITISH VICE CONSUL.

10/- CONSULAR SERVICE

BRITISH VICE CONSULATE ASTORIA OREGON

Sixteen pages.

Sophocles 1887 - 1888 Page 1

Eng. 1.

Executed in Sixteen Pages.

, Any Erasure, Interlineation, or Alteration in this Agreement will be void unless attested by some Superintendent of a Mercantile Marine Office, Officer of Customs, Consul, or Vice-Consul, to be made with the consent of the persons interested.

G. R. & R. O. RECEIVED 10 MAY 88 SHIPS R.N.R.

1888

AGREEMENT AND ACCOUNT OF CREW.

FOREIGN-GOING SHIP.

The term "Foreign-going Ship" means every Ship employed in trading or going between some place or places in the United Kingdom and some place or places situate beyond the Coasts of the United Kingdom, the Islands of Guernsey, Jersey, Sark, Alderney, and Man, and the Continent of Europe between the River Elbe and Brest inclusive.

Issued by the Board of Trade, May, 1880, in pursuance of 17 & 18 Vict. c. 104.

Name of Ship.	Official No.	Port of Registry.	Port No. and Date of Register.	Registered Tonnage. Gross.	Net.	Nominal Horse power of Engines (if any).
Sophocles	77455	Aberdeen	3 1879	1176	1119	

REGISTERED MANAGING OWNER. Name.	Address. (State No. of House, Street, and Town.)	No. of Seamen for whose accommodation is certified. (30 & 31 Vict. c. 124.)	Distance in feet and inches between centre of the Disc showing the Maximum load line in salt water and upper edge of lines indicating the position of the Ship's decks above that centre. First Deck above it. ft. in.	Second Deck above it. ft. in.
Wm Henderson	Aberdeen	32	4 – 6	—

Scale of Provisions to be allowed and served out to the Crew during the Voyage, in addition to the daily issue of Lime and Lemon Juice and Sugar, or other antiscorbutics in any case required by 30th & 31st Vict., c. 124, s. 4.

	Bread lbs.	Beef lbs.	Pork lbs.	Flour lbs.	Preserved Meat lbs.	Fish	Potatoes	Preserved Vegetables	Peas pint	Rice	Tea oz.	Coffee oz.	Sugar oz.	Molasses	Water qts.
Sunday	1	1½								½	⅛	½	18	2½	3
Monday	1	1½	¾							½	⅛				
Tuesday	1	1½	½							½	⅛	Daily			
Wednesday	1		1¼							½	⅛				
Thursday	1	1½	¼												
Friday	1									½	⅛	⅛			
Saturday	1	1½									⅛	⅛			

Note.—In any case an equal quantity of Fresh Meat or Fresh Vegetables may, at the option of the Master, be served out in lieu of the Salted or Tinned Meats or Preserved or Compressed Vegetables named in the above Scale.

SUBSTITUTES. NO SPIRITS ALLOWED

EQUIVALENT SUBSTITUTES AT THE MASTER'S OPTION

When 2 oz of butter or marmalade are issued daily the allowance of Beef or Pork [illegible] ... daily

The several Persons whose names are hereto subscribed, and whose descriptions are contained on the other side or sides, and of whom Two are engaged as Sailors, hereby agree to serve on board the said Ship, in the several capacities expressed against their respective Names, on a Voyage from[1]

London to Sydney & any Port or Places in Australia, New Zealand, India, China, Pacific, or Atlantic Oceans, West Indies, & America, trading backwards and forwards, as the Master may require, until the return of the vessel to a final Port of Discharge in the United Kingdom, calling at a Port for orders if required. Voyage not to exceed Two years

And the Crew agree to conduct themselves in an orderly, faithful, honest, and sober manner, and to be at all times diligent in their respective duties, and to be obedient to the lawful commands of the said Master, or of any Person who shall lawfully succeed him, and of their Superior Officers, in everything relating to the said Ship and the Stores and Cargo thereof, whether on board, in boats, or on shore: in consideration of which Services to be duly performed, the said Master hereby agrees to pay to the said Crew as Wages the Sums against their Names respectively expressed, and to supply them with Provisions according to the above Scale. And it is hereby agreed, That any Embezzlement or wilful or negligent Destruction of any part of the Ship's Cargo or Stores shall be made good to the Owner out of the Wages of the Person guilty of the same: And if any Person enters himself as qualified for a duty which he proves incompetent to perform, his Wages shall be reduced in proportion to his incompetency: And it is also agreed, That the Regulations authorized by the Board of Trade, which are printed herein and numbered[2] 1 2 3 4 & 7

are adopted by the parties hereto, and shall be considered as embodied in this Agreement: And it is also agreed, That if any Member of the Crew considers himself to be aggrieved by any breach of the Agreement or otherwise, he shall represent the same to the Master or Officer in charge of the Ship in a quiet and orderly manner, who shall thereupon take such steps as the case may require: And it is also agreed, That[3]

Twenty five hands all told are to be considered the ship's full complement of Crew

[4] The authority of the Owner or Agent for the allotments mentioned within is in my possession.

H. Hand [illegible] Superintendent, Officer of Customs, or Consular Officer.

[4] This is to be signed if such an authority has been produced, and to be scored across in ink if it has not.

In Witness whereof the said parties have subscribed their Names on the other Side or Sides hereof on the days against their respective Signatures mentioned.

Signed by Alexander Smith Master,

on the Twenty third day of August 1887.

These Columns to be filled up at the end of the Voyage.

Date of Commencement of Voyage.	Port at which Voyage commenced.	Date of Termination of Voyage.	Port at which Voyage terminated.	Date of Delivery of Lists to Superintendent.	I hereby declare to the truth of the Entries in this Agreement and Account of Crew, &c.
26th August 1887	London	21st April 1888	London	23 April	A. Smith Master.

[1] Here the Voyage is to be described, and the places named at which the Ship is to touch, or, if that cannot be done, the general nature and probable length of the Voyage is to be stated.
[2] Here are to be inserted the numbers of any of the Regulations for preserving Discipline issued by the Board of Trade and printed on the last page hereof which the parties agree to adopt.
[3] Here any other stipulations may be inserted to which the parties agree, and which are not contrary to Law.

N.B.—This Form must not be unstitched. No leaves may be taken out of it, and none may be added or substituted. Care should be taken at the time of Engagement that a sufficiently large Form is used. If more men are engaged during the Voyage than the number for whom signatures are provided in this Form an additional Form Eng. 1 should be obtained and used.

M. & Co. Ld. 5000 10-86

Sixteen pages

Sophocles 1887 - 1888 Page 2

PARTICULARS OF ENGAGEMENT

Reference No.	SIGNATURES OF CREW	Year of Birth	Town or County where born	If in the Reserve, No. of Commission or R V 2.	Ship in which he last served, and Year of Discharge therefrom. Year	State Name and Official No. or Port she belonged to	Date and Place of signing this Agreement. Date	Place	In what Capacity engaged, and if Master, Mate, or Engineer, No. of Certificate	Time at which he is to be on board
	1	2	3	4	5	6	7	8	9	10
1	A Smith (Master to sign first)	1840	Abdeen		1887	Sophocles	3 Aug	Glow	Master	
2	W. L. Clark	1846	Teignmouth		"	Avoimore Abdn	"	"	1 Mate	26 Aug
3	W. A. Ross	1862	Portsoy		"	Buckhurst Abbey	"	"	2 Mate	4 Aug Do
4	Charles W. Wood	1868	London		"	Sophocles	"	"	3 Mate	Do
5	Oskar Pettersen	1854	Christiania		"	Sophocles Abdn	23	"	1 Bosun	Do
6	William Barth	1860	Abdeen		"	Do	"	"	Carpenter	Do
7	James Mackland	1859	Do		"	Ballack Jeyle	"	"	Sailmaker	Do
8	Olav Nerem	1867	Banff 76390		"	Sophocles Dundee Abdn	"	"	Steward	Do
9	Alfred Hoch	1850	Gravesend			Do	"	"	Cook	Do
10	Jack Holmberg	1853	Stockholm			Northernbay	"	"	AB	Do
11	John Swensson	1854	Gothenburg		"	Electra Dundee Glow	"	"	AB	Do
12	Israel Swensson	1857	Lidkoping			Do	"	"	AB	Do
13	O J Jahnsen	1850	Christiania Drobak			Iron Bell	"	"	AB	Do
14	H Daily	1845	Glow		"	Herbourne Gpl	"	"	AB	Do
15	Wm Henry	1865	Do		"	Lady Jocelyn Abdn	"	"	AB	Do
16	H W Fox	1861	Bradford		"	Avoimore Glow	"	"	AB	Do
17	H Schmidt	1852	Germany		"	German Ship Abdn	"	"	AB	Do
18	George Redmore	1846	Bradford		"	Sophocles	"	"	AB	Do
19	Geo Houlden	1860	Lincoln			Aviemore Abdn	"	"	AB	Do
20	A Carlberg	1857	Karlshamn Sweden			Channel Queen Guernsey	"	"	AB	Do

† If any Member of the Crew enters Her Majesty's Service, the Name of the Queen's Ship into which he enters is to be stated under the head of "Cause of leaving"

* Engineers not employed on the Propelling Engines and Boilers

Ship Sophocles

64509 / 64548 | 42/7 | 5   24/11/87

Amount of Wages per Calendar Month (11)	Advance agreed to (12)	Amount of Monthly Allotment (13)	Signature or Initials of Superintendent, Consul, or Officer of Customs (14)	Date (15)	Place (16)	Cause (17)	Balance of Wages paid on Discharge (18)	Signatures of Crew (19)	Signature or Initials of Official before whom the Balance of Wages was paid and Release signed (20)	Reference No.	
			W. Bland	Remains in Command						1	38 6
8	1	4	MB	11/4/88	Ldon	Dis	27 15 10	W. D. Clark	WL	2	42
5	5		MB	"	"	"	27 3 6	W. A. Ross	Stream		
4 10			AS	"	"	"				4	28 6
4 5	4 5		MB	"	"	"	25 7 10	Oskar Petterson	WL	5	32 / 51
5 15		3	MB	"	"	"	19 2 10	W. Barratt	WL	6	12/5
4 10		2 5	MB	"	"	"	14 9 6	James Macklam	WL		57 / 14/5
5 10	5 10	3	MB	"	"	"	18 2 1	Alex Rivers	WL		23/5
4 5		2 2 6	MB	"	"	"	10 13 6	Alfred Shock	WL	9	22/5
2 10	2 10		MB X	9/1/88	Sydney	Deserted	N.S.			10	
2 10	2 10		MB	11/4/88	Ldon	Dis	13 14 6	John Swanston	WL	11	20/
2 10	2 10		MB	25/12/87	Sydney	Deserted	N.S.			12	
2 10	2 10		MB	21/4/88	Ldon	Dis	10 14 4	E. Johnson	WL	13	53 / 4
2 10	2 10		MB X	9/1/88	Sydney	Deserted	N.S.			14	
2 10	2 10		MB	21/4/88	Ldon	Dis	5 18 3	Wm. [illegible]	WL	15	509/5
2 10	2 10		MB	"	"	"	13 15 10	H. W. Fox	WL	16	26 / 7/5
2 10	2 10		MB	[illegible]/87	Sydney	Deserted	N.S.			17	
2 10	2 10		MB	21/4/88	Ldon	Dis	13 19 6	George [illegible]			
1 5	Discharged Sydney		MB	13/1/88	Sydney	Dis	1 17 6	Geo. Houlden	G. H. [illegible]		
1	1 5		MB	"	"	"	1 5	A. Calberg	G. H. B.		

should be described as Engine Drivers here and in Dis. 1.

"Discharged," "Deserted," "Left Sick," "Died."

X These desertions occurred after clearance hence the absence of the names from endorsement. A. Smith, Master

Sophocles 1887 - 1888 Page 4

4 *Name of*

PARTICULARS OF ENGAGEMENT.

Reference No.	SIGNATURES OF CREW.	Year of Birth.	Town or County where born.	If in the Reserve, No. of Commission or R V 2.	Ship in which he last served, and Year of Discharge therefrom. Year.	State Name and Official No. or Port she belonged to.	Date and place of signing this Agreement. Date.	Place.	In what Capacity engaged, and if Master, Mate, or Engineer, No. of Certificate.*	Time at which he is to be on board.
	1	2	3	4	5	6	7	8	9	10
21	George Heckmott	1867	Maidstone		1887	Stockbridge	23 Aug	Ldon	AB	26 aug
22	F. Greshwater	1855	Kent		"	Leila Ldon	"		AB	4 am D°
23	John Willson	1856	Dartford		"	Roma Bell	24	"	AB	D°
24	E. Hughes	1867	Ldon		"	Loch Lomond	23 Aug	"	OS	D°
25	J. Dorey	1867	D°		"	Pleiades Ldon		"	OS	D°
26	Arthur Smith	1870	Putney		—	First Ship	"	"	Boy	D°
27	James Beattie	1871	Abdeen		—	D°	"	"	Boy	D°
28	P. Hodgson	1871	Ldon		—	D°	"	"	Cooks Mate	D°
29	P Robinson	1873	Middlesbro		—	D°	5 Sept	Stowaway		
30	John Dines	26	Belfast			Jumna	5/1/88	Sydney	AB	9 am
31	James Johnstone	46	Glasgow			Parramatta	5/1/88	D°	AB	D°
32	John Campbell	29	Inverness			Star Lucia	5/1/88	D°	AB	D°
33	John Brown	40	Northampton			D°	6/1/88	D°	AB	D°
34	[illegible]	32				Waitomata	6/1/88	D°	AB	D°
35	Tukamoga	25	Japan			Professor Jamies	6/1/88	D°	AB	D°
36	William H. Foxy	24	Bath			Star Lucia	6/1/88	D°	AB	D°
37	J.W. Wyatt	19	Gloucester			Thomas Stephens	6/1/88	D°	AB	D°
38	Thos Goodhand	29	Yorkshire			Onyx	17/1/88	At Sea	AB	10 am 10 pm
39	Hugh Dow	30	Isle of Skye			Rosedale	17/1/88	At Sea	AB	10 am 10 pm
40										

* Engineers not employed on the Propelling Engines and Boilers

† If any Member of the Crew enters Her Majesty's Service, the Name of the Queen's Ship into which he enters is to be stated under the head of "Cause of leaving"

Ship *Sophocles* 5

Amount of Wages per Week, or Calendar Month.	Advance agreed to.	Amount of Weekly or Monthly Allotment.	Signature or Initials of Superintendent, Consul, or Officer of Customs.	PARTICULARS OF DISCHARGE, &c., To be filled in by the Master upon the Discharge, Death or Desertion of any Member of his Crew. Date, Place, and Cause of leaving this Ship, or of Death. Date.	Place.	Cause.†	Balance of Wages paid on Discharge.	RELEASE (late M). We, the undersigned Members of the Crew of this Ship, do hereby release this Ship and the Master and Owner or Owners thereof, from all Claims for Wages, or otherwise in respect of this Voyage. Signatures of Crew (each to be on the Line on which he signed in Col. 1).	Signature or Initials of Official before whom the Balance of Wages was paid and Release signed.	Reference No.	
11	12	13	14	15	16	17	18	19	20		
1	[illegible] Sydney		[illegible]	13/2/88	Sydney	Dis	1 ..	George Hicknott	[illegible]		
1	Do		[illegible]	Failed to Join						22	
1	Do		[illegible]	14/2/88	Sydney	Dis	2 7	John Willson	[illegible]		
1.10.	1.10.0		[illegible]	"	"	"	[illegible]	E. Hughes	[illegible]		
1.10.	1.10.0		[illegible]	"	"	"	[illegible]	J. Dorey	[illegible]	25	
1			[illegible]	21/4/88	Ldon	Dis	Nil	A Lewis	W L	26	
1			[illegible]	"	"	"	3 —	James Beattie	W L	27	
1	[illegible] Sydney		[illegible]	13/2/88	Sydney	Dis	Nil	P. Hodgson	[illegible]	28	
1	Do		[illegible]	26/12/87	do	do	Nil	with Officer	[illegible]	29	
4.10.	4.10.		James [illegible]	21/4/88	Ldon	Dis	10 6 0	John Davies	W L	30	5/5
4.10.	4.10.		[illegible]	"	"	"	10 12 0	~~[illegible]~~ James Johnstone	W L	31	4/5
4.10.			[illegible]	"	"	"	15 14 0	J. Campbell	W L	32	5/5
4.10.	4.10.		[illegible]	"	"	"	3 0 2	[illegible]	W L	33	5/5
4.10.	4.10.		[illegible]	"	"	"	9 5 0	[illegible]	W L	34	
4.10.	4.10.		[illegible]	"	"	"	10 6 0	[illegible] mark	W L	35	17/8/5
4.10.	4.10.		[illegible]	"	"	"				36	
4.10.	2.5.		[illegible]	"	"	"	6 6 6	J. W. Wyatt	[illegible]	37	
4 10	2 5.		A S	"	"	"	11 18 6	Thos Goodhand	W L	38	4/8/5
4 10.	4 10.		A S	"	"	"	9 11 9	Hugh Dow	W L	39	5/19
										40	

should be described as Engine Drivers here and in Dis. 1.
the Ship," thus, "H.M.S. Revenge," and the other Causes of leaving the Ship should be briefly stated thus, "Discharged," "Deserted," "Left Sick," "Died."

10 Name of

ACCOUNT OF APPRENTICES ON BOARD (IF ANY).

Christian and Surnames of the Apprentices at full length. 1.	Year of Birth. 2.	Registry of Indenture. Date of 3.	Port of 4.	Date. 5.	Place. 6.	Cause. 7.
Samuel Hollis Lews	1867	20.8.84	London	Failed to join		
Walter Robertson Marley	1870	7.10.85	Do		do	do Fever
Chas William Wood	1868	7.10.85	Do	21/1/88	Promoted to 3rd Mate. See Eng.	
Arthur Ball	1870	6.10.86	Do	Still by the Ship		
Benjamin Lenzell	1872	7.10.86	Do	18/1/88	Deserted at Sydney	
William John Brown	1870	20.8.87	Do	Still by the Ship		
Percy Sanderson	1867	3.11.85	Do		do	do
Walter R. Marley	1870	7.10.85	Do	Transferred from "Agrimore"		

X. This desertion occurred after clearance, hence the absence of the name on the Indorsement. [illegible] Master

CERTIFICATES

Or Indorsements made by Consuls or by Officers in British Possessions Abroad.

Engaged (8)

I hereby certify that I have sanctioned the Engagement of the following seamen viz. John Davies, Jas Johnston, J Campbell, John Brown, J Cambridge, J Kamaya, Wm H Fox and J.W. Wyatt upon the terms of the within written agreement, which they have signed in my presence.

Discharged (8)

I certify that the within written seamen viz. Geo Stoulken, A Carlberg, Geo Hickmott, J Willson, E Hughes, J Dovey, P Hopson, P Robinson have been discharged and left behind at this port on the grounds of mutual consent.

Deserted (2)

I certify that the within written seamen viz. Fred Swenson and H Schmidt have been left behind at this port as deserters and that a proper entry of such desertion in the official log has been produced to me.

[illegible]
Shipping Master
9/1/88

Soudan 1891 - 1892 Page 1

Executed in Sixteen Pages.

Eng. 1.

*** Any Erasure, Interlineation, or Alteration in this Agreement will be void unless attested by some Superintendent of a Mercantile Marine Office, Officer of Customs, Consul, or Vice-Consul, to be made with the consent of the persons interested.

Issued by The Board of Trade, Dec., 1890, in pursuance of the Mer. Ship. Acts, 1854 to 1890.

1892

RECEIVED 27 OCT 92

AGREEMENT AND ACCOUNT OF CREW.

FOREIGN-GOING SHIP.

The term "Foreign-going Ship" means every Ship employed in trading or going between some place or places in the United Kingdom and some place or places situate beyond the Coasts of the United Kingdom, the Islands of Guernsey, Jersey, Sark, Alderney, and Man, and the Continent of Europe, between the River Elbe and Brest inclusive.

Name of Ship.	Official No.	Port of Registry.	Port No. and Date of Register.	Registered Tonnage. Gross.	Registered Tonnage. Net.	Nominal Horse Power of Engines (if any).
Soudan	91182	Lpool	16 / [illegible]	1701	1699	—

REGISTERED MANAGING OWNER. Name.	Address. (State No. of House, Street, and Town.)	No. of Seamen for whom accommodation is certified (30 & 31 Vic. c. 124.)	FOR PARTICULARS AS TO LOAD LINE, SEE PAGE 13.
Jas McDonald	British Eastern Shipping Co 72 Bank R. Chrs. [illegible] Lpool	45	

Scale of Provisions to be allowed and served out to the Crew during the Voyage, in addition to the daily issue of Lime and Lemon Juice and Sugar or other antiscorbutics in any case required by 30th and 31st Vict., c. 124, s. 4.

	Bread lb.	Beef lb.	Pork lb.	Tinned Meats lb.	Soup and Bouilli pint.	Preserved Potatoes lb.	Compressed or Preserved Vegetables lb.	Flour lb.	Peas pint.	Rice lb.	Tea oz.	Coffee oz.	Sugar oz.	Molasses oz.	Water qts.
Sunday	1	1½						½			1/8	½	2		3
Monday	1		1¼						1/3						
Tuesday	1	1½						½							
Wednesday	1		1¼						1/3			Daily			
Thursday	1	1½						½							
Friday	1		1¼						1/3						
Saturday	1	1½													

Note.—In any case an equal quantity of Fresh Meat or Fresh Vegetables may, at the option of the Master, be served out in lieu of the Salted or Tinned Meats or Preserved or Compressed Vegetables named in the above scale.

SUBSTITUTES. No Grog. Lime Juice [illegible]

AT THE MASTER'S OPTION.

The Several Persons whose names are hereto subscribed, and whose descriptions are contained on the other side or sides, and of whom [illegible] are engaged as Sailors, hereby agree to serve on board the said Ship in the several capacities expressed against their respective Names, on a voyage from[1] Liverpool to Calcutta if required to any port or ports within the limits of 72 degrees North and 65 degrees South Latitude, trading to and from as any [illegible] of Continent of Europe between the River Elbe & Brest [illegible] calling for orders [illegible] of registered [illegible]

And the Crew agree to conduct themselves in an orderly, faithful, honest and sober manner, and to be at all times diligent in their respective Duties, and to be obedient to the lawful commands of the said Master or of any Person who shall lawfully succeed him, and of their Superior Officers, in everything relating to the said Ship and the Stores and Cargo thereof, whether on board, in boats, or on shore; in consideration of which Services to be duly performed, the said Master hereby agrees to pay to the said Crew as Wages the sums against their names respectively expressed, and to supply them with provisions according to the above Scale. And it is hereby agreed, That any Embezzlement or wilful or negligent Destruction of any part of the Ship's Cargo or Stores shall be made good to the Owner out of the Wages of the Person guilty of the same: And if any Person enters himself as qualified for a duty which he proves incompetent to perform, his Wages shall be reduced in proportion to his incompetency: And it is also agreed, That the Regulations authorized by the Board of Trade, which are printed herein and numbered[2] 1 to 4 are adopted by the parties hereto, and shall be considered as embodied in this Agreement: And it is also agreed, That if any Member of the Crew considers himself to be aggrieved by any breach of the Agreement or otherwise, he shall represent the same to the Master or Officer in charge of the Ship in a quiet and orderly manner, who shall thereupon take such steps as the case may require; And it is also stipulated that the Seamen shall receive the advances of wages entered herein against their names: And it is also agreed, That[3]

The said Master shall be entitled to deduct from the wages of the said Crew respectively the following amounts, viz.:—for not joining at the time specified in Column 10, two days' pay, or any expenses which have been properly incurred in hiring a substitute; and for absence from the Ship at any time without leave, a sum not exceeding two weeks' pay; and it is hereby mutually agreed, that any dispute arising on the subject of these deductions shall be settled by the Superintendent of a Mercantile Marine Office, Consular Officer, or Shipping Master abroad, and that his decision shall be final.

30 Hands all told are to be considered the ship's full complement of Crew.

No Cash shall be advanced abroad or liberty granted other than at the pleasure of the Master.

* The authority of the Owner or Agent for the allotments mentioned within is in my possession.
[illegible] Superintendent, Officer of Customs, or Consular Officer.
* This is to be signed if such an authority has been produced, and to be scored across in ink if it has not.

In Witness whereof the said Parties have subscribed their Names on the other Side or Sides hereof on the days against their respective Signatures mentioned.

Signed by Jas Donald Master,

on the 27th day of August 1891.

Date of Commencement of Voyage.	Port at which Voyage commenced.	Date of Termination of Voyage. (These Columns to be filled up at the end of the Voyage.)	Port at which Voyage terminated.	Date of Delivery of Lists to Superintendent.	I hereby declare to the truth of the Entries in this Agreement and Account of Crew, &c.
27.8.91	Liverpool	5.10.92	Hull	6.10.92	Jas Donald Master.[4]

[1] Here the Voyage is to be described, and the places named at which the Ship is to touch, or, if that cannot be done, the general nature and probable length of the Voyage is to be stated.
[2] Here are to be inserted the Numbers of any of the Regulations for preserving discipline issued by the Board of Trade, and printed on the last page hereof, which the parties agree to adopt.
[3] Here any other stipulations may be inserted to which the parties agree, and which are not contrary to Law.

N.B.—This Form must not be unstitched. No leaves may be taken out of it, and none may be added or substituted. Care should be taken at the time of Engagement that a sufficiently large Form is used. If more men are engaged during the voyage than the number for whom signatures are provided in this Form, an additional Form Eng. 1 should be obtained and used.

W B & L (251s)—787—7500-12-90

Sixteen Pages.

Soudan 1891 - 1892 Page 2

Name of

PARTICULARS OF ENGAGEMENT.

Reference No.	Signatures of Crew.	Year of birth.	Town or County where born.	If in the Reserve, No. of Commission or R. V. 2.	Ship in which he last served, and Year of Discharge therefrom. Year.	State Name and Official No. or Port she belonged to.	Date and Place of signing this Agreement. Date.	Place.	In what capacity engaged, and if Master, Mate, or Engineer,* No. of Certificate.	Time at which he is to be on board.
1	2	3	4	5	6	7	8	9	10	
1	Jas Donald	1842	Aberdeen		1891	Same			C 28188	
2	Master to sign first. Wm Kelk	/59	L'pool		9	do	24/8	L'pool	C 08.4.17 Mate	5 am 29/8/91
+ 3	Chas A. Potts	/53	St John NB		9	do	do	do	Bengal Pm. 164 2nd Mate	do
4	Alfred W. Emmett	/72	Dartmouth		9	do	do	do	Promoted as 2 Mate from 4/5/92 3rd Mate 02443	do
5	B Rosselien	/48	Christiansand		9	Roma L'pl	do	do	Carpr.	do
6	Richd Wilson	/63	Germany		9	Shuema "	do	do	Boatsn.	do
7	James Macklin	/58	Aberdeen		9	Sophocles	do	do	Sailmr.	do
8	John Night	/64	Jersey		9	Frankelint Aden L'pl	do	do	Stewd	do
9	Richard Lewis	/46	Holyhead		9	Smarina "	do	do	Cook	do
10	R. Meyrowsl	/70	Riga		9	Shuema "	do	do	AB NP	do
11	Tho Murray	/68	Bombay		9	do	do	do	AB NP	do
12	James Laan	/72	K'bright		9	Natuna Lpool	do	do	AB To 3rd Mate NP 4/92	do
13	J Johansson	/65	Finland		9	M & E Cann	do	do	AB NP	do
14	Emil [illegible]	/67	do		9	Gladstone NS	do	do	AB NP	do
15	Axel Ström	/70	Sweden		9	Roma NS Mport	do	do	AB NP	do
16	A Radmann	/69	Finland +		9	Shuema L'pl	do	do	AB NP	do
17	John E Jones	/65	Blackburn		9	Roma NS	do	do	AB	do
18	George Catterall	/45	L'pool		9	Bactria L'pl	do	do	AB NP	do
† 19	C Anderson	/43	Sweden x		9	B Crunchan	do	do	AB NP	do
† 20	August Fredrik	/62	Denmark +		9	Belford Grove [illegible]	do	do	AB NP	do

† If any Member of the Crew enters Her Majesty's Service, the Name of the Queen's Ship into which he enters is to be stated under the head of "Cause of leaving

* Engineers not employed on the Propelling Engines and Boilers

(257a)

Soudan 1891 - 1892 Page 3

Ship *Soudan* 3

Amount of Wages per Week or Calendar Month.	Advances made in the United Kingdom of not more than One Month's Wages, conditional on going to Sea. 12	Other Advances, not being conditional on the Seaman's going to Sea from the United Kingdom. 13	Amount of Weekly or Monthly Allotment.	Signature or Initials of Official before whom the Seaman is engaged. 15	PARTICULARS OF DISCHARGE, &c., To be filled in by the Master upon the Discharge, Death or Desertion of any Member of his Crew. Date, Place, and Cause of leaving this Ship, or of Death. Date. 16	Place. 17	Cause.† 18	Balance of Wages paid on Discharge. 19	RELEASE (see M). We, the undersigned Members of the Crew of this Ship, do hereby release this Ship, and the Master and Owner or Owners thereof, from all Claims for Wages, or otherwise in respect of this Voyage, and I, the Master, do hereby release the said undersigned Members of the Crew from all claims in respect of the said Voyage. Signatures of Master and Crew (each to be on the Line on which he signed in Col. 1). 20	Signature or Initials of Official before whom the Balance of Wages was paid and Release signed. 21	Reference No.
Monthly			Monthly								
[illegible]				Twr Emmott		Remains			Jas Donald	[illegible]	1
8 0 0	8 0 0			Twrl	7/10/92	Hull	Dischgd	72 12 4	N. Kolk.	IMH	2
5 5 0	5 5 0		2 10 0	Twrl	18/3/92	Calcutta	Disch	55 13 4	Chas A Potter	[illegible]	3
Wages 4 15 - per Month / 5 5 0	3 5 0			Twrl	7/10/92	Hull	Dischgd	35 18 9	A. W. Emmott	IMH	4
5 10 0	5 10 0			Twrl	"	"	"	62 10 8	R B Ramelean	IMH	5
4 0 0	4 0 0			Twrl	"	"	"	36 13 9	Richard Wilson	IMH	6
5 0 0	2 10 0		2 10 0	Twrl	"	"	"	32 4 4	James Macklin	IMH	7
5 0 0	5 0 0			Twrl	"	"	"	56 6 6	J. Night	IMH	8
4 10 0	4 10 0		2 10 0	Twrl	"	"	"	18 7 7	Richd Lewis	IMH	9
3 0 0	3 0 0			Twrl	"	"	"	29 7 1	R Meyton	IMH	10
3 0 0	3 0 0			Twrl	"	"	"	26 12 8	Thos Murray	IMH	11
5 / 3 0 0	3 0 0			Twrl	"	"	"	32 4 4	James Loan	IMH	12
3 0 0	3 0 0			Twrl	"	"	"	26 10 11	J Johanson	IMH	13
3 0 0	3 0 0			Twrl	"	"	"	29 15 6	Emil X Kormis	IMH	14
3 0 0	3 0 0			Twrl	"	"	"	29 11 11	Axel Ström	IMH	15
3 0 0	3 0 0			Twrl	"	~~Calcutta~~	~~Disch~~	28 10 8	A Radmager	IMH	16
3 0 0	3 0 0			Twrl	5/10/92	Hull	Dischgd	28 16 9	John E Jones	IMH	17
3 0 0	3 0 0			Twrl	"	"	"	30 4 3	Geo Catterall	IMH	18
3 0 0	3 0 0			Twrl	4/3/92	Calcutta	Disch	158 1 9	C. Anderson	HL	19
3 0 0	3 0 0			Twrl	"	"	"	132 - 1	A Frederiksen	HL	20

should be described as Engine Drivers here and in Dis. 1.
the Ship," thus, "H.M.S. Revenge;" and the other Causes of leaving the Ship should be briefly stated thus, "Discharged," "Deserted," "Left Sick," "Died."

(252a) Sixteen pages.

Soudan 1891 - 1892 Page 4

4 *Name of*

PARTICULARS OF ENGAGEMENT.

Reference No.	SIGNATURES OF CREW.	Year of birth.	Town or County where born.	If in the Reserve, No. of Commission or R. V. 2.	Ship in which he last served, and Year of Discharge therefrom. — Year.	State Name and Official No. or Port she belonged to.	Date and Place of signing this Agreement. — Date.	Place.	In what capacity engaged, and if Master, Mate, or Engineer,* No. of Certificate.	Time at which he is to be on board.
	1	2	3	4	5	6	7	8	9	10
21	I. A. Radstrom	1867	Finland		1891	Shucma [illegible]	27/1	Lpool	AB NP	5 am 29/8/91
22	Byron Dorr	1863	Portland		do	B Crunchan	do	do	AB NP	do
23	Benjamin Collins	1844	Jarmo[illegible]		do	Cabul Lpool	do	do	AB NP	do
24	Robert McCall	1849	Worken		do	Irvma Lpool	do	do	AB NP	do
25	A. Hamilton	1872	Tyrone		do	Same	do	do	AB NP	do
26	A. Edwardes	1873	London		do	do	do	do	OS	do
27	Kalon Lafferty	43	Dundalk			Ocone	16/5/92	Calcutta	W.B.	18/5/92
28	W. P. Simpson	48	[illegible]			Bengal	"	"	W.B.	"
29	Andrew Gilligan	32	[illegible]			Hope	"	"	W.B.	"
30	William Brown	19	[illegible]			Bengal	"	"	OS	"
31	W. A. Van nooten	85	West Indies			Hereford	"	"	OS	"
32										
33										
34										
35										
36										
37										
38										
39										
40										

* Engineers not employed on the Propelling Engines and Boilers

† If any Member of the Crew enters Her Majesty's Service, the Name of the Queen's Ship into which he enters is to be stated under the head of "*Cause of leaving*

(257a)

Soudan 1891 - 1892 Page 5

Ship *Soudan* 5

Amount of Wages per Week or Calendar Month. (11)	Advances made in the United Kingdom of not more than One Month's Wages, conditional on going to Sea. (12)	Other Advances, not being conditional on the Seaman's going to Sea from the United Kingdom. (13)	Amount of Weekly or Monthly Allotment. (14)	Signature or Initials of Official before whom the Seaman is engaged. (15)	PARTICULARS OF DISCHARGE, &c. To be filled in by the Master upon the Discharge, Death or Desertion of any Member of his Crew. Date, Place, and Cause of leaving this Ship, or of Death. Date. (16)	Place. (17)	Cause.† (18)	Balance of Wages paid on Discharge. (19)	RELEASE (late M). We, the undersigned Members of the Crew of this Ship, do hereby release this Ship, and the Master and Owner or Owners thereof, from all Claims for Wages, or otherwise in respect of this Voyage, and I, the Master, do hereby release the said undersigned Members of the Crew from all claims in respect of the said Voyage. Signatures of Crew (each to be on the Line on which he signed in Col. 1). (20)	Signature or Initials of Official before whom the Balance of Wages was paid and Release signed. (21)	Reference No.
3 0 0	3 0 0			Twod	4/3/92	Calcutta	Disch	161 - 10	T Rädman	HC	21
3 0 0	3 0 0			Twod	9/10/92	Hull	"	27 10 2	Byron Dorr	WC	22
3 0 0	3 0 0			Twod	4/3/92	Calcutta	Des	148 8 1	B Collins	HC	23
3 0 0	3 0 0			Twod	9/10/92	Hull	"	30 5 11	Robt × McCall	WC	24
3 0 0	2 0 0			Twod	"	"	"	29 19 2	A Hamilton	WC	25
0 10 0				Twod	"	"	"	- 8 6	A Edwards	WC	26
3 10 -	5 15 5			Hindquist	"	"	"	12 11 -	John Lappen	WC	27
3 10 -	5 15 5			HC	"	"	"	11 11 -	Wm B Simpson	WC	28
3 10 -	5 15 5			HC	"	"	"	12 5 0	Andrew × Milligan	WC	29
2 " "	3 16 6			HC	"	"	"	7 3 -	Wm Crone	WC	30
2 " "	3 16 6			HC	"	"	"	6 11 3	F. W. Van Hooken	WC	31
											32
											33
											34
											35
											36
											37
											38
											39
											40

should be described as Engine Drivers here and in Dis. 1.
the Ship," thus, "H.M.S. Revenge;" and the other Causes of leaving the Ship should be briefly stated thus, "Discharged," "Deserted," "Left Sick," "Died."

(252s) Sixteen pages.

Soudan 1891 - 1892 Page 6

ACCOUNT OF APPRENTICES ON BOARD (IF ANY).

Christian and Surnames of the Apprentices at full length. 1.	Year of Birth. 2.	Registry of Indenture.		Date, Place, and Cause of leaving this Ship, or of Death. *To be filled up by the Master.*		
		Date of 3.	Port of 4.	Date. 5.	Place. 6.	Cause. 7.
Alfred Nicholson	1874	19.2.89	Cardiff	24/9/92	at sea (10/92)	Slipped overboard & Drowned
James John Donald	1876	25.8.91	Lpool		Remain	
Wm Hy Montagu Wilson	1875	28.8.91	do			

CERTIFICATES

Or Indorsements made by Consuls or by Officers in British Possessions Abroad.

Soudan 1891 - 1892 Page 7

Ship____________________ 11

CERTIFICATES

Or Indorsements made by Consuls or by Officers in British Possessions Abroad.

Certified that the within undermentioned seamen have been discharged and left behind at this port on the alleged ground of mutual consent and that I have accordingly granted my sanction to their being so left and that their balance of wages paid to them and their effects delivered

J A Rodman	Rs 161	"	10	
A Frederickson	132	"	1	
B Collins	148	8	1	
C Anderson	158	1	9	
C A Potts	55	13	4	

Calcutta 18 March/92 H Lindqvist Dy Shipping Master

This Agreement was deposited in this Office on the 31st Jany/92 and is this day returned to the Master. The average rate of Exchange is at 1 - 3 7/8 per rupee -

Certified that I have sanctioned the engagement of the within named W. H. Lappin, W. B. Simpson, A. Milligan, W. Crane and W. G. Van Nooten upon the terms mentioned in the foregoing written Agreement and that they have signed the same in this Office with a full understanding thereof -

Calcutta 19th May/92 H Lindqvist Dy Shipping Master

GOVT. SHIPPING OFFICE CALCUTTA

I certify that in my opinion the entries in the Official Log confirmed by the statements of the Master + members of the crew respecting the death of Alfred Nicholson are true + correct + that no further enquiry is necessary in this case.

Hull 7 Oct 1892 J. H. Hogarth Dy Supt

(206a) Sixteen pages

Credits

University of Aberdeen - Museums and Special Collections,

The George Washington Wilson images, sourced from the Museums and Special Collections, University of Aberdeen, are provided under the terms of a Creative Commons Attribution 4.0 International Licence (CC BY 4.0). Each image shows the unique identifier number.

Dundee University

Images provided by Dundee University are reproduced courtesy of the University of Dundee Archive Services.

Google Maps

Google Map images are reproduced in accordance with their guidelines.

Lloyd's Register Foundation

The Lloyds Survey Reports of the ships are provided courtesy of Lloyd's Register Foundation.

The reports can be accessed on:
https://hec.lrfoundation.org.uk/archive-library

Trove

Trove is a website giving access to collections from Australian libraries, universities, museums, galleries and archives. It's free and available online.

The collection can be accessed on:
https://trove.nla.gov.au/about

State Library of Australia

Many of the photographs of the ships in Australia were sourced from the State Library of Australia, their unique identifiers are given with each image used.

The collection of images of clipper ships and Australian ports can be accessed at:
https://collections.slsa.sa.gov.au

Ian and Francis Fyfe, for assisting with the final draft.

Printed in Great Britain
by Amazon